Praise for

# THE BOOMERANG PRINCIPLE

## and LEE CARAHER

"The heart and soul of every company lies in its people. People bring brands to life and, ultimately, drive a company's success—but, they do not have to be within your walls to do so. Recognizing that everyone who interacts with your company has a hand in its success, is the new key to business sustainability. Buy and share this book, the benefits will boomerang back to you."

—Kevin Cleary, Chief Executive Officer at Clif Bar & Company

"Lee Caraher is one of the most able executives I know at making a place of work become the place to work. She values, coaches, and empowers her staff so that they give of their best while working for her and continue to give her their best even after they move on. This is what loyalty in today's economy looks like and has the power to propel careers and bottom lines. I have personally witnessed in my career the value created by welcoming and celebrating 'boomerangers.' I recommend leaders atop any organization pick this book up and put it to work."

—Dr. Jane E. Shaw, Board Member Yahoo!, Fmr COO ALZA, CEO Aerogen, and Board Member McKesson and Intel

"Lee Caraher marshals a compelling array of data on why employers should cheer on personal disruption even when it means people leaving where they are. Businesses need their people to grow and growing sometimes means moving on. If you're smart, you'll keep your employees close, and keep your former employees just as close!"

—Whitney Johnson, Thinker50, Author of *Disrupt Yourself* and *Dare, Dream, Do*

"'If you build it, they will come… back.' Okay, maybe not how the phrase goes, but still couldn't be truer. With her usual insight and pragmatism, Lee shows us the new definition of company loyalty and why we all need to start adopting it now."

—Richard A. Moran, Ph.D., President of Menlo College,
author of *The Thing About Work*

"The business landscape shifts rapidly; consider business ventures, product launches, mergers and acquisitions, and more. One thing we can control through all the movement is relationships with our people. People move too, but building relationships where they want to come back is not only the right thing but a powerful, long-term advantage. ***The Boomerang Principle*** is a smart and practical guide to making it happen."

—Scott C. Dettmer, Founding Partner at Gunderson Dettmer

"Having benefitted from a boomerang career myself, I speak with conviction. When your top performers love you, even when they leave they act as ambassadors like no other—spreading good words, referring good clients, and sending the best employees your way. Once again, Lee Caraher has nailed it ahead of common wisdom."

—John Boland, President and CEO, KQED Public Media

"My business premise is 'let's do it better.' And in this book, Lee offers us a way to do just that by better managing our ever evolving talent, creating a virtuous cycle of support, growth, and uncommon results. I recommend you jump on board now to get and stay ahead of the curve.

—Tom Kalinske, Chairman, Global Education Learning; Fmr CEO
SEGA, Mattel, Leapfrog

"Loyalty has changed. Lee, in her pragmatic and insightful way, shows leaders why and how to let millennial talent back in the door. Strike 'dead to me' from your vocabulary and share this great read with your managers today."

—Donald W. Derheim, Chief Executive Officer, SFJazz

"Understanding the new loyalty contract between employees and employers is crucial for any company seeking to build high-performing teams and achieve breakthrough results. Lee shows leaders why and then how to deploy this powerful rethinking of loyalty in organization to benefit the employee and employer alike."

—Kate Purmal, Former Senior VP SanDisk, COO Versaic Inc., and co-author of *The Moonshot Effect*

"This is a must-read for CEOs and CHROs of dynamic and fast-growth companies. Our workforce is changing and employers need to change the way they think about it. Our company is focused on creating great employee experiences for organizations and the 'Boomerang' topic is now becoming a standard part of the employee lifecycle discussion. These 'Alumni' are future business partners, social advocates, and often return as more experienced and valuable re-hires."

—Keith Kitani, Co-founder and CEO, GuideSpark

"In **The Boomerang Principle**, Lee has encapsulated what the best leaders and organizations already know; that talent is fluid and employees cannot be expected to stay with you forever. Lee demonstrates a clear blueprint for how the most successful organizations have embraced and leveraged their alumni to create value from these relationships and to leave the door open to a happy reunion."

—Robert Glazer, CEO, Acceleration Partners

"Loyalty is not dead! Caraher cuts through the stereotypes and myths associated with employee loyalty. What she shows us is loyalty, employee expectations, and business demands can indeed work together in mutually beneficial ways. Grab your highlighter and pen, you'll be marking up your book because so many nuggets of wisdom are in here!"

—Shawn Murphy, Author of *The Optimistic Workplace*, Founder/CEO of Switch+Shift

"Lee Caraher shares insights for leaders who want to maximize their return on investment in hiring talent. She provides compelling reasons and practical approaches to nurture talent in today's changing world of work. And of course, she brings her humor and personal touch to make this an enjoyable, smart read that you can put to use immediately in your organization."

—Willa Seldon, Partner, The Bridgespan Group

"Lee Caraher walks the walk when it comes to creating lifetime loyalty among her colleagues and employees. She takes great care of her employees—whether current or former—as she knows that investing in people isn't just the right thing to do, it also offers a payback to her and the company in spades. This book is a must-read for anyone who is part of an organization desiring to positively influence the world around them."

—Jeff Boehm, Executive Director at The Marine
Mammal Center

"*The Boomerang Principle* is a powerful articulation of how the fundamentals of outstanding organizational culture and leadership are critical determinants of a company's performance. And it links these fundamentals to the advantages of being open to rehire employees. This is a valuable guidebook for any leader wanting to maximize their personal contribution to their company's ongoing success."

—Mark Perry, Strategic Advisor, Retired General Partner
at New Enterprise Associates

"Lee is the best Silicon Valley has when it comes to working with the next generation and creating a humane and effective workplace. No one can beat her intelligence, humor, common sense, and just plain wisdom."

—The Rev. Dr. Malcolm Clemens Young, Dean
of Grace Cathedral

"Lee's approach to leadership works across the board, regardless of sector, industry, or company size. As Lee explains in her book, engagement is about people and understanding that loyalty is a shared bond that the right leadership can help create. Lee lays out a powerful case for why every organization should care and then she gives us the tools to get it done. I highly recommend her book for any organization dependent on lasting, loyal engagement of the people it touches."

—Bryan Neider, Chief Executive Officer at Gatepath; Former Senior Vice President, Global Operations, Electronic Arts

"Everyone understands the concept of Lifetime Customer Value. What Caraher advocates for eloquently is as important and revolutionary: Lifetime Employee Value."

—Eric Roos, CEO Nancy Boy

"Over the years, I have watched Lee hire young people with great promise, coach them to greatness, graciously support their leaving to spread their wings elsewhere...and then welcome them back to the Double Forte fold. Inevitably these employees return with new knowledge, expanded abilities, and renewed appreciation for the caring culture of learning, excellence, and service Lee promotes. There is no better employee retention program!"

—Lori Ogden Moore, Executive Coach, OM Associates

# THE BOOMERANG PRINCIPLE

LeeCaraher.com    @leecaraher    #BoomerangPrinciple

# THE BOOMERANG PRINCIPLE

Inspire Lifetime Loyalty from
Your Employees

## LEE CARAHER

bibliomotion
inc.

First edition published in 2017
by Bibliomotion, Inc.
711 Third Avenue New York, NY 10017, USA
2 Park Square, Milton Park, Abingdon, Oxon OX14 4RN, UK

International Standard Book Number-13: 978-1-62956-168-4 (Hardback)
International Standard eBook Number-13: 978-1-3152-1276-0 (eBook)
International Standard Book Number-13: 978-1-62956-170-7 (Enhanced eBook)

**Library of Congress Cataloging-in-Publication Data**
Names: Caraher, Lee, author.
Title: The boomerang principle : inspire lifetime loyalty from your employees / Lee Caraher.
Description: New York, NY : Routledge, 2017. | Includes bibliographical references and index.
Identifiers: LCCN 2016048734 | ISBN 9781629561684 (hardback : alk. paper)
Subjects: LCSH: Organizational behavior. | Corporate culture. | Loyalty. | Employee motivation.
Classification: LCC HD58.7 .C3476 2017 | DDC 658.3/14—dc23
LC record available at https://lccn.loc.gov/2016048734

**Visit the Taylor & Francis Web site at**
**http://www.taylorandfrancis.com**

Printed and bound in the United States of America by Sheridan Books, Inc. (a Sheridan Group Company).

*For Pete*

# Contents

# Acknowledgments

First and foremost, thank you to my husband, Pete, and my children, Michael and Liam, also known as my biggest fans. Your love and support are immeasurable; you are why I do what I do.

A special thank you to all the people who have worked with me in my different companies more than once (or twice, or three times!), especially Dan, Liz, Maggie, Michelle, Bill, and Heather: We have proven together that the great ones always come back and that together we can make our work even better. I appreciate your trust in me, your dedication to your own great careers, and your willingness to experiment to forge a different, more positive way forward. It is humbling to be among you.

Thank you to the hundreds of people who have spent their valuable time with me to help inform my writing—your e-mails, conversations, notes, comments, and interviews have been invaluable, and your insights will be helpful to anyone who reads this book. To my mother who blazed incredible trails and who inspires me from beyond more and more the older I get, and my father whose sense of humor, incredibly high standards and belief in me makes its mark every day—thank you.

Many thanks to Jill, Erika, Alicia, and Susan of Bibliomotion and to Michael and the fabulous team at Taylor and Francis; I'm honored to be among your chosen authors. Finally, to my Chix—you know who you are—your support & friendship is everything.

# INTRODUCTION

*"They're dead to me." "I'm not going to spend all this time training them just to have them leave." "They're job-hoppers who don't know a good thing when they see it." "I'm on a constant training revolving door—as soon as someone's trained up, they're out, and I have to start all over again." "Why am I wasting my time? It'll be faster if I do the work myself."*

I can't tell you how many times I've heard these sentiments from entrepreneurs, CEOs, managers, and supervisors over the past three years in my work helping companies create positive intergenerational teams, organizations, and workplaces of all sizes. I can't tell you, because I stopped counting. I'd set out to answer the questions these people and companies had about Millennials, Gen Xers, Boomers, and Traditionalist Generation members working together well, and I'd end up addressing a deep-seated resentment about the perceived lack of loyalty shown by employees to their colleagues and employers.

The disconnect is palpable, and the consequence of the resentment is debilitating to businesses of all sizes across the country.

My personal journey on loyalty—or "hanging on to people," as I think of it—began during the dot-com boom in the late 1990s. I had started an integrated marketing communications firm for one of the big three international media/marketing agencies in San Francisco, which was ground zero for the dot-com boom. Right when Gen Xers, a generation almost half the size of the Boomer (and now Millennial) generation, were coming into the job market, money was flooding into online businesses, and everyone in Silicon Valley seemed to be in an arms race for talent given that spawning, scaling, and then either selling, acquiring, or IPOing as fast as possible was the name of the game. Our firm's business was driving awareness for our clients among customers, consumers, and, most importantly, potential investors to increase the perceived value of the client through media and expert coverage of the companies with which we were on retainer. Frankly, given the vast amount of capital flowing into dot-com businesses, which in turn drove the race for awareness-induced valuations, if you had a pulse, you got a job.

As I grew the practice, my office became a revolving door of people who'd been offered new jobs with higher salaries and who wanted me to counter. At first I did, scared to lose revenue-generating people when I had big numbers to bring home for HQ; without people I couldn't make my numbers. The result was an increasingly contentious workplace where colleagues questioned one another's value, plotted to get more, and felt they were being screwed. Everyone knew we would cave to an employee's demand for more money, vacations, or perks when she presented other offers in hand, and employees seemed be waiting their turn to either test the boundaries or cast scorn on those who did. It sucked.

One morning, I woke up exhausted and said "Enough." I decided I wasn't going to counteroffer anymore. I was going to focus on the people who were doing their jobs and looking for opportunities to grow, not those who were planning to leave for more money, and screw it if I didn't make my numbers—none of my peers were making their toplines either without a huge hit to their net profit. Let them walk me out of a happier workplace. I felt lighter and more rested immediately.

I didn't even have time to roll out my decision to my leadership or the rest of the company before I got a chance to put it into action. That week, the first person who wanted me to counter, post-epiphany, came into my office to tell me that he had a new job. I said to him, "Good luck." He was incredulous. "Aren't you going to counter me?" "No," I said, "your head is already out of here, and I'm not going to pay you more for less of your brain. How can I help you?" And I proceeded to give him some pointers for working with his new company. The ripple was fast and positive. While that young man did indeed leave (and left that next job quickly), other employees responded to the news of "no more counters" first spread by that fellow, and then reiterated by me at the next staff meeting, with what I like to think was a palpable breath of relief. People stopped demanding counters, and our leave rate dropped. My numbers went up.

That started a new way of thinking for my staff and me. We would focus on making our organization the best it could be with the belief that environment and culture would translate into a better workplace, which would translate into better work and better business. Instead of just showing people the door, we'd actively help them find what was next and welcome people back to us if they wanted to rejoin, we had the right position for them, and we had had a good conversation about expectations this time around. While the dot-com bust curtailed our ability to actually bring anyone back to that company, my own company, Double Forte, began in 2002 with a handful of people who had worked with my cofounder and/or me in the past; what I call the *Boomerang Principle* has fueled our business from the beginning, with many employees returning for a second employment, referring clients and other employee candidates, and becoming clients.

Of course, I am not the first to base a business model on exiting people successfully. Consulting companies McKinsey, Bain, and Deloitte, among other long-standing strategic consulting firms, all have long traditions of helping place thousands of employees with clients or other companies, and these people then extend the consulting contracts and services with their previous employer; it's a key revenue driver. These former employees "boomerang" as clients or referrals. Intuit, LinkedIn, eBay, PayPal, Xactly, and many others all have a good history of boomerang employees—people who left and then returned to serve in either new or expanded roles. Beyond this, some of the highest-profile CEOs have been or are Boomerangs; these include Howard Shultz of Starbucks, Brad Smith of Intuit, Tim Westergren of Pandora, and the most famous, Steve Jobs of Apple.

Some companies have come to understand that former employees need not be the enemy and can, in fact, be their biggest allies, collectively. These companies have built apparatus and adopted a mind-set that supports employees in crafting their own careers and returning to serve as employees or contractors at different times with different, enhanced skill sets.

These companies are a small minority, however. Many still operate from the point of view that employers deserve the loyalty of their employees simply because the companies pay those people. Despite the dramatic shift in employment expectations that happened as fallout from the economic meltdown in 2008 and the resulting Great Recession, many companies have not shifted to the reality that they helped create with the massive downsizings that occurred in 2008 through 2011.

As Stanford researchers Jeffrey Pfeffer and Peter Belmi have noted, "The daily news provides numerous cases of companies not repaying employee loyalty and, instead, harming employees and ex-employees through their actions."[1] Indeed, the notion that there's a new employee–employer equation is strong and readily visible in workplace articles from across the country. Eilene Zimmerman encapsulates the commonly held belief that things have changed when she writes, "There was a time in the not-so-distant past when the American workplace operated under an implicit agreement: Employees who worked hard at their jobs and stayed loyal to their company were rewarded with job security, health benefits and other perks."[2]

Employees today, particularly Millennials (born 1980–2000) know that they need to craft and actively manage their own career paths and that staying fresh and relevant is vital to a long and prosperous work life. Employees don't expect to stay in a position or company for long by Boomer and Traditionalist standards, and they will actively seek positions that promise opportunity if their aspirations are not realized meaningfully in their current position. Millennials are conscious of creating their own brands because their parents have drilled into their heads that they can't count on a company to take care of them. Gen Xers (born 1965–1981) are in the middle of careers that are looking longer than they anticipated, and many older Boomers are hoping to hang on until retirement, which seems to get pushed out further and further every year. People seem to understand that they can't count on finding that "I'll retire from here" position their parents and grandparents may have enjoyed.

## Generations at a Glance

| | |
|---|---|
| Generation Z | Born 2001–2019 |
| Millennials | Born 1980–2000 |
| Generation X | Born 1981–1965 |
| Baby Boomers | Born 1946–1964 |
| Traditionalists | Born 1945–1925[3] |

At the same time, 46 percent of Millennials indicate that they would absolutely consider returning to a former employer[4]—a huge positive delta compared to Gen Xers and Boomers, only 33 percent and 29 percent of whom, respectively, would consider returning to work at a former employer, even if they'd left on positive terms.

While some might say this indicates that Millennials are leaving their companies too soon, it may be simply because they do not consider tenure a positive or relevant factor in their career trajectory. Or, it may be that some Millennials' disappointment in the reality of work compels them to leave a job instead of trying to work it out. I have pages and pages of examples of that, but try to remember that I'm hearing these stories of what I would call unrealistic expectations and job abandonment through my older ears. What some people call entitlement, I call conditioning.[5]

Millennials, in general, have grown up hearing about work–life balance virtually their whole lives, thanks to the Boomer and Gen X

xxii                                  Introduction

working women who have paved more hospitable and flexible work lives for themselves and those behind them. In addition, Millennials have had the power of "instant access" to people, companies, and institutions in their hands for much of their lives. Their opinions have been solicited and sometimes compensated early and often by product companies that are eager to capture their purchasing power. And with the disintermediation of media, Millennials have grown up in a culture in which influence has been distributed much more widely and talent has emerged in many fields outside of the traditional business models, career paths, and "processes." Boomers and Gen Xers, on the other hand, came to understand "how things were done." While certain individuals of any generation may be entitled, Millennials as a generation are not; they simply have different expectations of their experiences based on the advantages the proliferation of technology has afforded them.

Yet many companies—of all sizes—have yet to shift to a mind-set or philosophy that leverages the new equation between employers and employees. Indeed, 60 percent of the people I interviewed and surveyed across the country indicated that their companies either had strict policies or unspoken, but well understood, rules against rehiring former employees, regardless of how great they were in their previous positions. And in a recent survey, half of companies either still have or recently abandoned a policy against hiring boomerang employees "even if the employee left in good standing."[6]

## The Old Way

Michael Bloomberg is often cited for his firm stance against hiring former employees. Bloomberg, like a lot of founders, describes a business world consisting only of "us" and "them." But his conception includes a third class of characters, for whom he reserves a special circle of hell. Call them "those who used to be us"—the people who, by leaving Bloomberg's company to work elsewhere, have contravened his code of loyalty. He won't rehire them. He won't permit a good-bye party. He won't even—if he can help it—shake their hands. "Why would I?" he asks rhetorically. At a juncture in management-science history when the old social contract between employer and employee has been judged a museum piece, and when every worker is urged to think like a "corporation of one," Bloomberg is a throwback. Loyalty, he's convinced, is everything.[7]

Small- to medium-sized companies are particularly hard hit with the new employer–employee relationship, which has a large impact on the economy and the general condition of work around the country. Most people in this country, and indeed the world, do not work for large companies with sophisticated human resource departments. According to the U.S. Census Bureau, while large enterprises (those with more than five hundred employees) employ a small majority of American workers (51.6 percent in 2012), 99 percent of U.S. establishments with payrolls have fewer than 250 employees. Firms with fewer than one hundred employees have the largest share of small business employment; very small enterprises—companies with fewer than twenty people—employ almost 20 percent of the American workforce.[8] This does not count the self-employed who aren't incorporated. Millions of people work for companies run by teams who wear many hats and may not have had the bandwidth or wherewithal to keep pace with the dramatic business and cultural changes that have occurred in the last decade while they worked to stay afloat.

At the same time, the rise of the contract economy—with the success of companies such as Uber, Lyft, Upwork, Fivvr, Care.com, Varsity Tutors, TaskRabbit, and so many others that offer Internet platforms that match independent contractors with specific skills to the companies and solopreneurs that need them—brings an entirely new dynamic to people's professional expectations and opportunities and to companies' searches for reliable and consistent talent to deliver on their business. We are in the early days of a dramatic talent and service market shift, yet I predict that those platform companies that engender loyalty from their talent pool rather than their users will be the most successful in the long term.

I've never met an Uber driver who wasn't also a Lyft driver, and I've found the same graphic designers on Upwork as on Fivrr—no individual will rely on one platform to help him bring home the bacon, real or vegan. Businesses that can create marketplace demand for a particular service while honoring the actual provider will ultimately be those to which the talent pool is loyal. And without the personal connection or contract implicit in actual employment, loyalty will be predicated almost entirely on the platform company's ability to deliver.

Where does all of this leave us?

Boomerangs—people who remain loyal to companies, not just people, after they leave—are now important drivers of sustainable business models for organizations for all sizes. Companies need to shift their philosophies, business practices, and mind-sets to embrace and leverage the fact that Americans increasingly understand that they will have to create their own careers and retirements; therefore, companies will only flourish when they engender and earn loyalty in their employee or talent bases so that when (not if) they leave, employees or contractors will boomerang back as customers, referrers, advocates, or employees for their lifetimes.

Boomerangs are the drivers of sustainable business.

In addition to drawing on my own experience, I draw on interviews with more than one hundred business leaders—people who've returned to former employers (as well as those who wouldn't consider it)—and surveys with more than five thousand participants to share collective learning on creating a constructive work alumni group that may include boomerang talent. In the following chapters, I share how to put the Boomerang Principle to work for your business or team. Loyalty is not dead! The loyalty contract has changed, however, and when we embrace our new reality, we can dramatically improve our workdays, careers, and bottom lines.

# CHAPTER 1

# The New Loyalty Paradigm

"No one's loyal anymore; why should I invest one minute in these people? They're all going to leave soon anyway." So began my conversation with a general manager of a Boston-based medium-sized technology firm; I'd asked, "What's your biggest pain point right now?" And his response is a variation on a theme I've heard over the past five years in my work as the CEO of my own company, board member for a variety of nonprofit organizations, member of Entrepreneurs' Organization, and keynote speaker on creating positive intergenerational workforces. Boomer bosses, in particular, seem to have a difficult time with the reality that their younger colleagues, especially Millennials, don't plan to stay in one company for a very long time. Or at least their perception is that Millennials won't stick.

Loyalty—the quality or state of having a strong feeling of support or allegiance to a company or organization[1]—has long been equated with the tenure of an employee. No more. In today's world, where people expect to chart their own meaningful careers independent of a set time at any one entity, we need to shift our definition of loyalty to a company from a long tenure to a lifetime of allegiance regardless of employment status.

What businesses small, medium, and large need today is a proportional growing army of former employees who remain advocates, consumers, and friends of our companies. This is the future of the thriving workplace: Successful companies will inspire valuable alumni who ensure their businesses' relevance and vitality. We need boomerang employees who come back to our companies as consumers, referrals, partners, clients, contractors, and, yes, employees for a second or third tour of duty.

> The Boomerang Principle: the belief that organizations that allow and encourage former employees to return have a strategic advantage over those that don't.

Those companies that shift now for the long game of allegiance will have a strategic advantage over those that don't. Why? First, because this mind-set, and the actions, policies, and cultures that derive from it, actually keep good employees in companies longer than they had planned, which in turn drives efficiency and profit. Second, returning employees become fully functional and utilized exponentially faster than new employees. Third, the larger your allegiant footprint, the more sustainable your business will be.

## Millennials: Job-Hoppers?

"Why are Millennials such job-hoppers?" This question has been almost universal in my work coming out of *Millennials & Management: The Essential Guide to Making It Work at Work*, the book I wrote out of my experience recovering from what I called my company's epic failure to retain Millennials. More than 150 interviews and 50 speeches and workshops later, I can tell you that the lament of "no one's loyal anymore" is an important, and damaging, narrative—or background music—in companies of all sizes across the country today. Search *job-hoppers* or *job loyalty*, and you could spend hours just paging through the results, most of which are laden with negativity.

> Job-hopping isn't new, we just haven't learned how to deal with it efficiently and positively.

Job-hopping isn't new to most Boomers or Gen Xers. We've conveniently forgotten the late 1990s, when many Gen Xers were entering a hot job market. At that time, as the dot-com bubble economy seemed to double in size every week, the common refrain was "if you've got a pulse you've got a job," and as soon as graduates got jobs, they quickly got recruited to other ones. Then, the numbers were in the Gen Xers' favor; the economy was expanding just as the smallest generation, Generation X's 46 million to the Boomers' 78 million, was graduating from college. There just weren't enough young people to fill the ranks of companies in almost every sector.

## My Boomer Job-Hopping Career

I was born in the last year of the baby boom generation, and by today's definition I would be called a job-hopper. The longest job I've had is as CEO of my own company. My resume reads like that of a job-hopper of today: I had a string of three one-year stints, then three years, two and a half years, nine months, three and a half years, two and a half years (where I boomeranged back to my fourth job), and then fourteen years as the founder and CEO of Double Forte. Job-hopping is not new; we just haven't learned how to deal with it efficiently and positively.

The job-hopping bonanza of the late 90s was short lived, however. The Gen X workforce has been struck twice at critical career junctures by ill-timed economic events that have greatly impacted their career trajectories.

When the dot-com bubble burst in 2000, the impact on the economies in tech-heavy regions around the country, including the San Francisco Bay Area, Seattle, New York, and Boston, was negative and profound. Then, the aftermath of 9/11 in 2001 created further economic compression in many other sectors across the country. In the San Francisco Bay Area alone, more than eighty thousand professionals left the region to find work in other states; there simply wasn't enough work. Gen Xers (who were between twenty-two and thirty-six in 2001) were at the beginnings of their careers when this huge compression occurred.

Indeed, I started my company in 2002, and in that job-scarce, talent-rich environment, I found that I could easily staff my company with contractors who had ample experience and worked for *very* reasonable rates.

I had left my previous job six weeks after 9/11, determined to spend my days doing work I loved with people I liked. The revolving door of young Gen X colleagues, coupled with an exploding economy and then the reality of the contracting business environment in 2000 and 2001, had left me disenchanted. Most of my time was spent either trying to keep butts in seats on the upswing or get them out in the downturn, all without losing any revenue. In my own company, I could control who worked for me and who we worked for.

So, my business partner and I decided we wanted to avoid working with the young, demanding Gen Xers who represented most of our management issues over the previous four years, and we only hired people with at least ten years of experience, which took us out of the majority of the Gen X talent pool in 2002.

And, of course, the financial collapse of 2008 and the ensuing Great Recession happened right as Gen Xers were finding their career strides and dramatic earning potentials again and as Boomers by the hundreds of thousands were planning to retire. More than 8.8 million Boomers[2] and Gen Xers lost their jobs between 2008 and 2010. And the last seven years have represented a struggling, irregular rebuilding of the economy as millions of older Boomers have been hanging onto their jobs as long as possible to rebuild their retirement savings, Gen Xers are hitting middle age, and Millennials are entering the job market like a tsunami.

And here's the rub: Millennials have flooded into the workplace in the millions since 2010, moving into a challenging economy where far older colleagues are wanting to claw back their retirement funds. But the Millennials don't seem to stick at the jobs they've landed. While the reality of the Great Recession remains a significant dynamic for Boomers, who now face increased difficulty finding and keeping work and/or saving for their retirements, as well as for many Gen Xers, the oldest of whom have just entered their fifties, Millennials seem to be job-hopping. This is the case even when 36 percent of working Millennials live at home and 71 percent of students graduating from four-year colleges have significant debt.[3] The average debt is rising for public, private, and for-profit colleges, where the average debt at graduation is $25,500, $32,300, and $39,950, respectively.

Margo, CEO of a mid-sized advertising firm, shares her exasperation: "It is so frustrating to have worked so hard to keep my company not just alive but actually growing in the last five years and have Millennials just walk out the door when they don't like what it is to work. What did they think work was supposed to be?" This is a sentiment I heard over and over again in my interviews with executives across the country.

The generational difference in attitudes toward work can be stark, and it creates frustration, at the least, and resentment and distrust, at the worst, from people who have been through the economy-driven career wringer.

Not that it's been easy for all Millennials to find work. The oldest set of Millennials—those born between 1980 and 1987—have, for the most part, been able to find jobs. The middle group, the largest cohort of Millennials, is where the real pain point in this generation lies. Millions of these Millennials born between 1988 and 1996, have had a stunted start to their careers given the fallout of the Great Recession, and they are still trying to catch up to where they "should be" based on their education. Job-hopping for this group seems antithetical to their experience to most Boomers, Gen Xers, and older Millennials, and the perception is that Millennials aren't loyal to their employers, despite how challenging it has been to find work. Yet, here we are.

My friends and I feel that we're 'behind.' Most of us didn't get our first 'real jobs' until three or four years after college.
    —Sara, a twenty-nine-year-old retail executive from St. Louis

According to the Bureau of Labor Statistics, the average worker today stays at each job for 4.2 years down from 4.6 years in 2014.[4] The longitudinal view on these numbers is, of course, drastically interrupted by the 8.8 million people who lost their jobs between 2008 and 2010. The reality is the reality, and we have to deal with what is instead of what we wish were true if we're going to focus on building sustainable businesses staffed by people who know they have to be their own best advocates.

The breakdown among gender, generation, and sector is extremely revealing. In January 2014,[5] the median employee tenure for men was 4.7 years, while women had a slightly shorter tenure of 4.5 years. Among men, 30 percent had ten years or more with their current employer, while 28 percent of women had the same longevity. For Boomer workers fifty-five to sixty-four years old, 10.4 years was the median tenure. Among older Boomers, those sixty to sixty-four years of age, 58 percent were employed for at least ten years, compared with only 12 percent for older Millennials ages thirty to thirty-four. Millennials in the twenty-five to thirty-four age group had a three-year tenure median in 2014. And the public sector had nearly double the tenure longevity, at 7.8 years, as the private sector, 4.1 years. Interestingly, 75 percent of government workers were over thirty-five years old, while 60 percent of commercial business workers were over thirty-five years old. (The implications—positive and negative—of the large difference between private and government tenure deserve a closer look, but that's a different book.)

## A Long Time Coming

The shift in "loyalty" among workers has been building for many years. Much like the proverbial frog in water over a flame, we are just waking up to the fact that the water is at a high simmer today, and if we want a chance for a more positive understanding, we need to act now. We need to jump out of the hot water, or we will find ourselves and our businesses increasingly irrelevant—and not at an incremental rate, but at an exponential one.

Older people I interviewed, those fifty-five and older, talked about workplace loyalty as "normal" for them. They believed that if they worked hard and stayed at their companies, they would be "taken care of" with retirement plans and health insurance.

As executive coach and leadership expert Ray Williams explained in *Psychology Today*, "In the work world where employees were lifetime workers and employers took care of them, that concept of loyalty made sense. However, today's work world is vastly different: lifetime employment doesn't exist, and employers, including governments, have reneged on their promises."[6]

Employees are driving the shift in loyalty because they know that they can't count on one company—any company—to provide for them. While Boomer bosses may lament the "fall of loyalty," they too know that they can't count on the company to stay loyal to them; the last ten years of labor statistics have proven this fact over and over again.

In response to a blog post by popular serial entrepreneur and career guru Penelope Trunk before the 2008 meltdown, one commenter, Ken, noted, "Attitudes about company and employee loyalties are definitely changing. My own father worked thirty-five years for one company. I followed his lead and worked twenty-five years for one company but they went through a corporate merger and eliminated my department. So I tried again with another company and stayed ten years. This second company bought out a competitor and eliminated the group I worked in. I am now working for a third company but feel NO loyalty to this company and doubt that I ever will. I followed my father's work ethic but I tell my daughter to be cautious about becoming too loyal to any one workplace."[7]

This shift really started in the 1980s, when companies started laying off vast numbers of employees in order to achieve better margins and investor returns. [8] Healthy businesses were driving profit, and they started "rightsizing" their organizations to deliver payoffs to Wall Street and increase shareholder value. As Adam Cobb, a Wharton management professor explains, companies that announced staff layoffs would say,

"We are doing this in the long-term interest of our shareholders." Indeed, the 1980s saw the beginning of the trend to push the cost of long-held sacrosanct benefits such as pensions and health care to their employees; workers went from defined benefit plans to 401(k)s, and they were expected to assume larger and larger copays while employers paid a smaller share of health-care premiums.

Another commenter on Trunk's blog posted: "Please, employees aren't loyal because they know their employers can—and will—lay them off at the drop of a hat . . . entirely due to forces completely outside of the employee's control. If employers want more loyalty, they shouldn't be slaves to the next quarterly earnings report from Wall Street."[9] Remember, this comment was posted *before* the economic meltdown of 2008–2009. And this sentiment has only increased among workers since that time.

Pressure from investors for quarterly returns started a snowball of short-term employment actions that broke the implied contracts between companies and their workers. No longer was it good enough to work hard and be rewarded for a job well done. The norm is now work hard and deliver quarterly profit goals or perish. This trend in publicly traded companies has damaged the long game for total business return.

In one survey of corporate executives of publicly traded companies, none of the participants said that they would invest in a five- to ten-year plan guaranteed to increase profitability if it meant "a penny off of their share price." The reason, according to one CEO? Because "the market would kill me. Activist shareholders would kill me," and then the company would have to spend enormous time and energy "fending off this attack." Clearly, today's corporate interest for publicly held companies is not in the long term, and therefore, they cannot, by definition, prioritize their employees in the equation.[10]

The implosion of financial markets in 2008 and the ensuing Great Recession put the final nail in the coffin of the implied contract between employees and companies. The 8.8 million people who lost their jobs in the Great Recession, most without regard to tenure, feel the loss keenly. According to the Center for Work-Life Policy, the number of employees who trust their employers fell from 79 percent to 22 percent between June 2007 and December 2008.[11]

A scene from *The Big Short*, which chronicles how three investors identified and then capitalized on the housing bubble and resulting economic meltdown in 2008, captures a telling moment of this final breakdown in employee job loyalty.[12] As a manager projects loudly over a flood of employees exiting Lehman Brothers on September 15, 2008, "Go directly to your transportation and don't talk with the press," the audience can hear an angry and, I would say, scared employee yell back, "So that's it?! After eighteen years, I just leave? That's . . . great. I'll talk to whoever the hell I want."

In the recovery, many Boomer job seekers have found that they aren't considered "relevant" to the future of work and can't command the job titles, responsibilities, or salaries their careers previously pointed toward. Their resumes and skill sets are "stale" and "old," or else they are "overqualified" and "too experienced" for the jobs at hand.

## Loyalty and the American Dream

The state of the American dream has a lot to do with the dissonance between employers who value and seek loyalty and are disappointed, or even angry, when they don't receive it and employees who may or may not believe in a correlation between work and the American dream.

Many definitions and criteria are loaded onto people's different interpretations of the American dream, and indeed the meaning of the American dream has ebbed and flowed over time and among people of different demographics and cultural and social backgrounds. However, if we focus on the "hard work" element, some interesting and relevant themes emerge that can help us understand how our culture has shifted and how we as employers can work with the current trends to help our employees achieve their career and life goals.

Pulitzer Prize–winning writer and historian James Truslow Adams wrote the defining characterization of the American dream in his 1931 treatise *The Epic of America*, an international best seller. His book and his definition became foundational to American civics studies across the country and are still referred to today in middle and high school classes. About work, Adams writes: "Life should be better and richer and fuller for everyone, with opportunity for each according to ability or achievement" regardless of birth. So he advocates for ability and achievement in a world unfettered by privilege determined by status, birthright or wealth, and he believes that application determined equals realization of opportunity.

Contemporary American cultural historian Lawrence R. Samuel, author of many books and writer of *Psychology Today's* column "Psychology Yesterday," explains further how deeply the American dream is seated in our collective conscious: "For many in both the working class and the middle class, upward mobility has served as the heart and soul of The American Dream, the prospect of 'betterment' and to 'improve one's lot' for oneself and one's children is much of what this country is all about. 'Work hard, save a little, send kids to college so they can do better than you did, and retire happily to a warmer climate' has been the script we have all been handed."[13]

The equation of working hard and being rewarded is ingrained in our culture and propagated around the world. A 2015 story in the *Atlantic* titled "Who Still Believes in the American Dream?" chronicles the thoughts of a wide range of Americans and immigrants on the American dream.[14] The immigrants who writer Chris Arnade talked with were unilaterally optimistic believers in the dream. One recent Mexican immigrant living in New Mexico captured this optimism in his comments about hard work in America: "I am living the American dream. I have a job, a family, and my son goes to a great school, and if he works hard enough, he can have any job he wants. I didn't have that. He does. That is a dream come true."

Throughout the story, the phrases "work hard," "good job," "if you work hard enough, you can get what you need," and "work hard and live free" refer repeatedly to the correlation between hard work and a good life.

A poll commissioned for the Eleventh Aspen Ideas Festival revealed that "more than six in ten Americans believe the Dream can best be accomplished with hard work, compared with only 28 percent who say 'circumstances of birth' and 11 percent who say 'luck.' "[15] However, Boomers aged fifty-one to sixty-four in 2015 are the most disillusioned regarding the promise of the American dream. In the same study, statistically significant negative gaps persist between this group and other age groups in terms of their pessimism "about their future" and whether they are living, or can live, the dream.

In my own research, this generational divide played out along similar lines. In general, the Boomers I've interviewed fall into two camps, disillusioned and pragmatic, but both camps seem to agree that what they thought growing up is a fallacy; which group you fall into is determined by whether you think you got sold a bill of goods or were just naïve.

The implicit contract of the American dream—if I work hard, I will be rewarded—relied on corporate America to hold up its end of the contract: to reward hard work. Today's Boomer and Gen X workers have lived through one, two, or three downturn reminders that companies need not reward hard work. Today, the American dream is weighted more on the individual carving his or her own path through work. The new mantra is: work hard, don't count on the firm for the long term, and chart your own career independent of one company. So while a majority of Americans, newly minted or with families that have been here for generations, may still believe in the American dream, their confidence that employers will live up to their part of the equation is low.

## What Happened to the Gold Watch?

The gold watch retirement celebration, once part of the ritual of employment and retirement, is now a distant memory for Boomers and an anachronistic reference for Millennials (who don't even wear watches)[16] if they know the reference at all, as fewer and fewer of their own parents are receiving those symbols of a career well done.

Yet, many, many companies and their management staff act as if lifetime employment remains the modus operandi of the day and expect that their employees to be loyal to them; these companies have yet to shift their expectations to the reality they created.

# CHAPTER 2

# The Evolution of Loyalty
## From Company to Self to Both

When I am talking with business owners or managers about employee loyalty, the biggest complaint I hear is, "No one's loyal to their employers any more—they're just loyal to themselves. They're a bunch of job-hoppers who are always looking for that next best thing for themselves." When I first started working with companies struggling with intergenerational conflict, the divides were often stark, and comments were negative and excessively judgmental. And even now, with three years under my belt spreading the good word about Millennials and about how Boomers, Gen Xers, and Millennials can all work, relate, and have fun together, I'm still apt to get negative responses when I ask specifically about Millennials. Sometimes, I see more negativity than ever; clearly, my work is not done.

As a report from the Wharton School stated, "If loyalty is defined as being faithful to a cause, ideal, custom, institution or product, then there seems to be a certain amount of infidelity in the workplace these days."[1]

That's a big *if*.

Loyalty to self and company need not be either bound by employment or mutually exclusive.

Loyalty is a two-way street, and unless a company can prove to employees that it deserves their loyalty, it isn't coming. Frankly, the business world has taught us all that we need to be loyal to ourselves first if we don't want to be caught on the wrong side of a downsizing.

People are more loyal to their careers than to their employers. Whereas previous generations may have stuck it out until a raise was granted, younger workers may not have the patience to do so.[2] When managers point out that employees prioritize their careers over the company's well-being, I say, "Of course they do." And they should.

Employees know that the companies they work for are not islands, and they cannot control all that is around them. Mergers, acquisitions, and disruptive business models and technologies proliferate in today's business environment. The great job you do today may ensure that you don't have a job tomorrow. Or, your good work may be meaningless when a business or industry is turned upside down by changing dynamics completely out of its control.

We are in an incredible moment of straddling many contrary—almost irreconcilable—dichotomies: "traditional" business models and new disruptive ones that don't respect the way things used to be; multigenerational workplaces with colleagues divided by age, technology, and expectations; and world economies that impact local business. What used to work doesn't seem to work—and then it does again. We are at moment of incredible confluence, where stability of business is not ensured and divining the future feels more like shaking a Magic 8 Ball than traveling a sure path. And we will continue to be at this confluence for the next ten to fifteen years. Our seemingly topsy-turvy environment has colored Millennials' views of their employers and their responsibilities for their own careers. At one end of the spectrum, employee sentiment tends toward the skeptical and cynical: "The company you work for is not supremely worried about your well-being, and it's definitely not your friend."[3] At the other end of the spectrum is employees' awareness that no one company will be able to provide all the opportunities they want over the course of their careers, and that what's important is giving 100 percent to a company during one's tenure.

As Shawn Murphy, author of *The Optimistic Workplace*, said to me in an interview, the new definition of loyalty means "I will give you

1000 percent while I'm here. But if the business doesn't allow me to have meaningful work and lead a life that is important to me, then I won't stay very long."[4]

In her aptly titled article "Your Employer Is Not your Friend, and Young People Know It," Nikelle Murphy (no relation to Shawn) writes, "Just as employees are a resource for a company, younger generations of workers are beginning to view companies as stepping stones in their careers."[5]

Dharmesh Shah, founder and CTO of Hubspot, an inbound marketing software platform company, touched a real nerve when he published "7 Qualities of a Truly Loyal Employee." On LinkedIn, where Shah has more than 650,000 followers, his post got high traction, with almost 1,500 comments. He wrote, "Where employees are concerned, loyalty has nothing to do with blind obedience, or unthinking devotion, or length of tenure," and he went on to describe his seven-point checklist. Why is Shah's definition different? Because Hubspot values getting things done; it prefers high performance to longevity. Shah's is a much more transactional view of contribution.

"Think of it this way," Shah writes. "Which employee displays greater loyalty? 1. The employee who has been with you for ten years and in that time has learned to do just enough to fly, unseen, under the performance issues radar or 2. The employee who has been with you for 18 months and believes in where you're going, how you want to get there—and proves it every day by her actions. Of course experience is important, but given the choice I'll take the employee behind door #2 every time."[6]

Hubspot is well known in marketing and start-up circles for its "cult like" climate or its "lovable culture," depending on your point of view.

Dan Lyons, a former *Newsweek* reporter, creator of the extremely popular "Fake Steve Jobs" blog, and a writer for the HBO series *Silicon Valley*, wrote of his experience working at Hubspot in *Disrupted: My Misadventure in the Start-Up Bubble*. In it he describes his view of the Hubspot "bro" culture almost dripping from the manifesto. "Hubspot's Culture Code: Creating a Lovable Company," what the company calls "the operating system that powers Hubspot," is part manifesto, part employee handbook.[7] The code has been viewed more than 2.9 million times on SlideShare the popular presentation hosting platform owned by LinkedIn as of September 2016.

In his book, Lyons describes with incredulity the company's process of "graduating" employees whenever someone quits or gets fired. "Nobody ever talks about the people who graduate, and nobody ever mentions how weird it is to call it 'graduation.' Everyone acts as if all these things are perfectly normal."[8]

Several current and former Hubspottees came to the company's defense after the book was published, including Lauren Holiday, who had contracted for the company's nonprofit Inbound.org and penned a commentary in *Fortune* magazine titled "Working for This Startup Wasn't Hell—You're Just Old."[9] Others hopped on Lyons's bandwagon.

The whole body of work is worth a read as an example of two extremes: on the one hand, a fifty-plus Boomer journalist who'd been replaced by much younger reporters in a *Newsweek* rightsizing now working in a fast-paced, IPO-driving start-up dependent on fast-working, low-paid employees and contractors, the vast majority of whom were much younger than him; on the other hand, Millennials and other "new economy" workers embracing a new model with vastly different expectations from their older colleagues. The lenses through which each side viewed the same environment are so different one might think they didn't work at the same organization. Neither extreme is representative, although I found the book captured the stereotypes that abound and is laugh-out-loud funny to people like me who work with the same kind of companies. The truth of the future is in the middle, I think.

In the end, companies do not exist for the sole benefit of their employees, no matter the rally cry management uses to inspire or demonstrate its commitment to employees.

As Dawn Rasmussen writes in *Careerealism*, a career advice and job search magazine, "Don't forget, for even one moment, the workplace is first and foremost a business environment, and your being there is a mutual business decision."[10] Businesses exist to serve a customer's need, and over time customers' needs change. To continue to meet those needs, companies need to constantly evolve. While change may have taken place over a decade or two or three at the beginning of our older colleagues' careers, it is now happening so fast we can see it day by day. And what was once a relevant skill set may be completely obsolete in a company today.

This rapid shift has been hard for many Baby Boomers to accept. It wasn't that long ago that the rewards system was based on long tenure and not just achievement, but that equation has fallen apart given the new math that pervades our twenty-first-century economy. Young employees know this; they've had it drilled into their heads by parents caught flat-footed in 2008 and by friends who haven't found work commensurate with their expectations or their education. Many of these young people will seek a constantly evolving work environment ripe with opportunities to learn and advance.

## The Oprah Effect

Oprah gets a lot of credit for "making" a company—or a book or product the company makes—simply by naming it to her list of favorites. In my business representing clients to the media and other influencers, it used to be that nothing was more coveted for a consumer product company than being on an "Oprah's Favorites" show or on the "O List" in the magazine. Oprah's producers, reporters, friends, and friends of friends stave off relentless efforts from PR professionals all over the world to get their clients' products in front of Oprah.

Translucent Chocolates was catapulted to the national stage in 2008 when it was added to the O List. Founder Annastacia Hubbard described the impact of getting her chocolates in front of, and then endorsed by, Oprah as "transformational."

"Being on the O List was an immediate catapult in multiple ways, and just as they had warned me, we had almost a thousand orders the first day and five thousand orders within two weeks," Hubbard said. And that success continues today.

I think Oprah's bigger impact is on the tens of millions of people she has inspired to align their careers with their values and self-understanding. While the rise of self-actualized careers shaped by individuals who actively and vocally seek work that matters to them has obviously been influenced by the actions of companies that act on behalf of their shareholders in the short term, Oprah's impact cannot be underestimated, even though it may not be measurable. I believe that Oprah Winfrey has had an incredible and indelible impact on people's—mostly women's—career aspirations, which has changed the career equation for tens of millions of employees, entrepreneurs, and business leaders throughout the country.

Her message—you are responsible for your life—is not new. However, she used her incredible platform, the center of which was *The Oprah Winfrey Show*, with its twenty million daily viewers, to sear this message into the psyches and hearts of her huge audience.

> You are responsible for your life. If you're sitting around waiting for someone to save you, to fix you, to even help you, you're wasting your time, because only you have the power to take responsibility to move your life forward. And the sooner you get that, the sooner your life gets into gear.
>
> —Oprah Winfrey

As a black businesswoman from the Deep South without money or access, Winfrey is without peer as a standard bearer for the power of personal responsibility and finding purpose and happiness through effort and awareness. And her longevity in the business means that generations of people have not just felt but have absorbed her message.

In the context of her passion for education, Oprah's message has been delivered and celebrated by some of the most prestigious colleges in this country, including Harvard, Stanford, Duke, Howard, Spelman, National, and Johnson C. Smith, to name a few. Her speeches at corporate conferences, awards ceremonies, and her own "The Life You Want Weekend" have inspired millions of people to start ventures, take more control of their careers, and demand more from their time awake.

> But the challenge of life I have found is to build a résumé that doesn't simply tell a story about what you want to be but it's a story about who you want to be. It's a résumé that doesn't just tell a story about what you want to accomplish but why. A story that's not just a collection of titles and positions but a story that's really about your purpose.[11]
>
> —Oprah Winfrey

Josh Rosenberg, cofounder and CEO of Day One Agency, a New York-based digital communications firm, explained the "pretty big impact" Oprah, whom he has never met, has had on his career:

> For me, what stands out the most in terms of my own life is Oprah's focus on the power of positive thinking. She would talk about envisioning the end result, keeping a positive attitude, and working hard to get to the end goal. As the CEO of my company, I've applied this thinking to my team and incorporated a "good vibes only" mantra in the office (both figuratively as well as literally, hanging a sign with the words on our wall).
>
> Oprah regularly discusses the impact Maya Angelou has had on her own life, and one such quote she highlights is "When someone shows you who they are, believe them." As someone who works in a client services industry, I'm regularly meeting new personality types and making assessments on how potential business relationships might unfold.
>
> A few years ago, when I was just starting my own company, I had a meeting with a prospective client and red flags went off in my head about this person's expectations and work style. Oprah's Maya Angelou quote was in the back of my head the entire time.

While I discussed the situation with my business partners afterward, we decided to take the business for a number of reasons. However, the client ended up being exactly like I thought in the first meeting. And now, I listen to that voice and believe who's talking from the first time they show who they are.

I could fill this book with stories of people who felt inspired by Oprah to start companies or take different paths in their careers. More than three-quarters of the women I interviewed for this book answered the question "How much influence do you think Oprah Winfrey's message has had for you?" with "Very much."

Is it any surprise that Millennials have coalesced these simultaneous streams—the economy, their parents' reality, and cultural influence—to embrace a narrative of work that matters, a career that is fulfilling and self-directed, and a desire to make an impact at and through work?

## Loyalty in the Gig Economy

The gig economy—an environment in which temporary positions or short-term project assignments are common and organizations contract with independent workers for short-term engagements[12]—is all the rage. They may be raging for or raging against, depending on the industry sector (drivers, artists, programmers, handy people, etc.), the state, and the mechanism through which people find temporary work. And the gig may be as temporary as a car drive across town or as extended as a multiyear virtual assistant relationship.

A comprehensive study conducted in 2010 by Intuit predicts that by 2020, 40 percent of American workers will be contract employees who have no traditional employers.[13] The McKinsey Global Institute's 2016 report *Independent Work: Choice, Necessity, and the Gig Economy* sized the U.S. population of independent workers at 20 to 30 percent, or fifty-four million to sixty-eight million working-age people.[14]

## Independent Workers

Today's independent workers:

- Have a high degree of autonomy with a high degree of control and flexibility in deciding their workloads and work schedules
- Are paid by the task, assignment, or sales performance, not by time spent working
- Have short-term relationships with their customers, the people or companies that pay them for their services

—Adapted from *Independent Work: Choice, Necessity, and the Gig Economy*, McKinsey Global Institute, 2016

Independent workers, giggers, or free agents, as they may variously be called, come in many forms determined by their circumstances and preferences. McKinsey Global Institute breaks independent workers into four categories:

1. **Free agents**—people who choose to be independent and whose incomes are based solely on contracts. Free agents make up about 30 percent of U.S. independent workers, approximately twenty-two million people.
2. **Casual earners**—workers who, by choice, augment their salaries with supplemental income from short-term contracts. This is the largest cohort in the U.S., at 40 percent of independent workers. There are about twenty-seven million casual earners.
3. **Reluctants**—people who would prefer to have full-time employment but who "derive their primary income from independent work." Reluctants represent 14 percent of independent workers, about ten million people.

4. **Financially strapped**—people who make ends meet with additional income from independent work because their compensation from their employment doesn't pay the bills. The financially strapped make up another 14 percent, or nine million independent workers.[15]

The biggest shift for independent workers, digital marketplaces that match workers with work and provide the means for payment, have just started to make an impact in free agent and gig contract work. These markets, steered by technology-driven platforms that pair people seeking work for hire and people needing work done, are growing quickly, spreading globally, and offering a wide range of business models. Yet, despite tremendous media attention and coverage dedicated to the companies offering these platforms and their business practices, only 15 percent of independent workers in 2016 have used online marketplaces "to earn income."[16] Obviously, the potential for worker/task market places is tremendous.

It's too early to say how it will all shake out—except to say that Uber, UpWork, Fivrr, Lyft, Task Rabbit, Thumb Tack, Handy, Mechanical Turk, and the myriad other platforms will all probably undergo a few business model transformations before regulations, laws, and user preferences are sorted out.

In the end, competition abounds, and no one platform will exist in any one market. Ultimately, the value of the platform will be in the quality of the work product, and, in the most simplistic way of thinking about it, the quality of the work product depends upon the people doing the work. The best workers will seek the best platforms, and platforms will require the best workers to deliver on their brand promises. So it behooves the workplace platform providers to do everything they can to capture the loyalty, affinity, and allegiance of their "working members" (you can't call them workers unilaterally) to ensure that the most revenue possible goes through their platforms.

The gig economy is still in its early days, and if these companies don't want a race to the bottom, they will place more emphasis and care on the people fulfilling the work than anything else. Differentiation will come from the way these platforms manage to command the best providers at the most valuable price.

At the same time, giggers in the United States need to ensure that they are constantly upping their games and making themselves as relevant and valuable as possible. In a search on Upwork, MyVirtualWorkforce, and Freelancer.com, virtual assistants in South Africa, Malaysia, and the Philippines all provided comparable skill sets and abilities to their American counterparts at much lower costs per hour. In addition, they work hours opposite those of the typical U.S. workday, which means we can go to sleep having stacked up work for a virtual assistant and turn our computers on the next day with all that work completed.

The worldwide economy is changing dramatically for the knowledge worker. Experience is not enough to ensure growing competitive compensation. The men and women who competed at a set rate for the assignment I offered included people from different countries, of different ages, and with a wide range of experience. I've learned how to sort through the queries to yield the people best suited for my assignments, but I have chosen between workers over age fifty and under age thirty for the same assignment at the same rate. It feels very much like the fast-food-ization of knowledge and skill work, where everyone at the counter makes the same wage, regardless of experience. Loyalty, from the consumer's point of view, is expressed by a five-star rating and good tips; from the gigger's point of view, it's too soon to call.

### Gig Bridge Jobs People Like

One Lyft driver I had said "I quit my job at Salesforce because it was too much work and they couldn't fill the open recs, so there was no end in sight and I couldn't move up since my department was so understaffed. I'm doing this so I can meet people and network to find my next job while I make money." I volunteered that he probably shouldn't lead with "Salesforce is too much work" if he wanted to find a new job quickly, and wished him well.

And while gig platforms promise workers the freedom and flexibility to work how and when they want, giggers do not control the platform, the competition, or the flow of work, and, in the end, the dynamic may not benefit U.S. independent workers.

## The Most Loyal Act: Loyalty to Self and Company

Loyalty to self is not a zero-sum game for companies and organizations. It is possible for employees to be loyal to a company and to themselves simultaneously. Loyalty is a two-way street, and it must be earned . . . both ways. And employees need not be employed continuously to be loyal, just as companies can extend their appreciation for service well rendered past the termination date.

### Nicole's Story

Nicole worked at my company, Double Forte, for seven years. A vice president, she was a key member of our leadership team and the lead on several key accounts. Our relationship transcended employer–employee; we are friends. Near the end of her time with the company, the nature of her work changed; she was tired; we were changing business models; and it wasn't fun for her anymore. She resigned.

I didn't want to listen. I wanted Nicole to take a month or two off and then come back refreshed and ready to roll. She considered it, talked it over with her husband, and resigned again. I accepted it this time. After a well-deserved break, Nicole started her own consultancy, and Double Forte refers clients we are too large to service to her regularly.

She was so right. She needed to leave to pursue the life she wanted. The most loyal thing she ever did in seven years of great work was to resign when she knew that Double Forte couldn't provide her with the opportunity she wanted. We remain friends, and she provides a great sounding board for other employees and myself. She is also a vocal advocate for Double Forte.

Loyalty means leaving when you are no longer motivated.

The most loyal act an employee can do is to leave when he is no longer interested or motivated by his work or the opportunities available at the company. As much as it's the person's responsibility to *drive* his career and not assume that he doesn't need to actively manage it, it is also his responsibility to leave when he is no longer *engaged*, productive, or happy.

The most sustainable businesses now and for the future are the ones that have former employees who remain loyal over their lifetimes—they boomerang back to the companies on their resumes in many ways over a period of decades. Business owners, managers, and supervisors have a tremendous opportunity. The shift we need to make is from begrudging employees' "early" departures and realizing that mutually beneficial loyalty to self and the company is not just possible, it's business and career building. With this mind-set, organizations can shift their energies from negative to positive and work to ensure that former employees are lifelong advocates for their organizations.

# CHAPTER 3

# Personal and Talent Brands at Work

Loyalty to self *and* company is the new desired equation that working people and organizations need to seek for the most rewarding careers and the most sustainable businesses; it's an equilibrium balanced between people who are proud to be associated with a company and companies that are proud to employ great people. While companies still have the power of the paycheck, their abilities to attract and retain the best people, either as talented employees or contractors (both those who wish to be employed and those who wish to remain separate), will increasingly determine sustainability and profitability in competitive markets.

Of course, being known as a great place to work is not a new advantage in the marketplace. Tremendous resources have been dedicated to "employer branding"—creating abundant, positive awareness for companies, teams, or departments as personally rewarding, exciting, compelling, and/or lucrative career destinations. Public or company relations professionals, internal or external, dedicate millions of dollars of effort to getting on to—and then staying on—highly regarded "Best Places to Work" lists published by high-profile industry, regional, special interest, or national publications. Indeed, editorial segmentation among best-of lists—by category (best places to work for parents, women, people of color, English majors), by size (small, medium, large, international), or by industry (best tech, consulting, PR, advertising, health care, etc.)—generates a significant editorial footprint every year.

However, the changing dynamics of recruiting and retaining the best employees that have emerged in the recovery from the Great Recession have flipped the emphasis in employer branding from being a great place to work to being a place where great people work. This seemingly subtle but actually very dramatic shift in emphasis—from employer to employee, or talent—is a result of a confluence of dynamics. First is the widespread impression that companies were breaking their implied promises to their long-term employees by not keeping them on the payroll until retirement. Second is the explosion of the Internet economies—Web 1.0, 2.0, etc.— which have fundamentally changed long-standing business practices and the relationships between employers and their employees and customers. The third dynamic that contributed to the shift from employer to employee is the rise of personal empowerment fostered by Oprah, Tony Robbins, and a long list of self-help gurus in the past twenty years.

Companies now must embrace themselves as "talent brands" that are known not only for their products and services but, as importantly, for their ability to hire and develop exceptional people who are proud to be associated with their employers.

The rise of personal branding, necessitated in many ways by the widespread impression that companies were breaking their implied promises to their longtime employees and fostered by the idea that people should be responsible for their own career success, has ironically or serendipitously created a dramatic new pressure on organizations. In this framework, we need to think of our organizations as the bumper stickers of a resume, icons that tell the story of the person who puts them on their CV for everyone else to see.

Employers are the bumper stickers of a resume.

## The Brand of You

Tom Peters, best-selling author and management guru, has significantly influenced modern business with what has been described as "the best business book of all time," *In Search of Excellence*, which he coauthored with Robert Waterman in 1982. Peters is credited with articulating and propelling momentum for the concept of personal branding in his 1997 *Fast Company* article "The Brand Called You."[1] In this prescient article, he exhorted his readers to "take a lesson from the big brands" such as Nike, Starbucks, Champion, and Levi's and brand themselves in order to stand out. At the beginning of the explosion of Internet business—what he called "the new world of work"—he knew that "to be in business today, our most important job is to be the head marketer for the brand called You."

Peters and Waterman's article is amazing to read twenty years later, not just because of the 20/20 vision afforded by time or the words you never see today, such as "Rolodex" and "the Net," but also because of how clear the authors' crystal ball was about how our business world would evolve and their keen understanding of the power of personal influence, which today we work to leverage every day in marketing, politics, customer service, and product development. Peters's book, *The Brand of You*, was published two years after the *Fast Company* article, and today remains a top-ranking book on Amazon.

Peters started a movement of personal branding that is just now, twenty years later, really taking hold almost unilaterally among knowledge workers worldwide. Daniel Pink, another well-respected and often-quoted consultant of the "new way of working," codified personal branding in his first of many best sellers, *Free Agent Nation*, in 2001, describing the future of self-employment as one in which free agents move from contract to contract. Today, we call this the "gig economy," and many experts predict that by 2020 more than 50 percent of all jobs will be held by contractors rather than employees.

More recently, high-profile authors Dorie Clark and Whitney Johnson, as well as experts Chris Brogan and Gary Vaynerchuk, have "modernized" the concept of personal branding with their books, blogs, and videos. An Internet search today for "personal branding" will yield more than 5.8 million entries; more than 120 online courses about how to create personal brands on Udemy, the popular online course platform; and more than ten thousand presentations on SlideShare. What started with a 3,500-word article in a niche business publication has mushroomed into a content-rich field with too many data points to count. Add to this the call of Oprah, Tony Robbins, and other influencers who advocate taking personal responsibility for happiness and purpose, and factor in the consequences of the Great Recession, and you have twenty years over which the culture has evolved toward a collision of personal brands in today's workplace.

## Creating and Maintaining Your Personal Brand

Your personal brand is what other people say about you when you're not there. Of course, what you produce and publish or say drive the response, so creating a platform—even a small one—that you own and control is critical in the social media age. You may not be able to control what people say about you, but you absolutely can and should control what you say about yourself through words, images, video, and audio.

### Own Your Name

Today, with social networks, apps, chatbots and other yet-to-be-developed important platforms, the most important thing you can do is to claim your name when new widgets pop up. Presenting a unified moniker across platforms is step one to being able to manage the brand that is you online. Even if you don't have plans to use the different platforms right now, claim your name on them so that someone else doesn't. At the very least, create profiles for LinkedIn, Twitter, Facebook, Instagram, SnapChat, About.me, Pinterest, and Skype. Having your name spelled the same way as an e-mail address before the @ sign across e-mail platforms also helps create a strong online brand for yourself.

## Create a Destination for Potential Employers, Partners, or Clients

At the minimum, create a strong LinkedIn profile, complete with well-written descriptions of your strengths and experience. List any nonprofit or volunteer work that you do as well. Better yet, take the next step and create a website with your name, or something close to it, as the URL. You don't need to be a coding jockey to create a good website; use Wix.com, SquareSpace.com, or Wordpress.com. Be sure to include a contact page with an e-mail or phone number where people can reach you.

## Consider Your Photo

Choose a well-composed photograph to use in all your professionally facing online profiles, such as LinkedIn and Twitter. Consider paying for a professionally shot image. What should you wear? Solid colors; no patterns or stripes. Choose a wardrobe that projects an image of yourself as you want your next employer or client to view you.

## Be Helpful

Valuable personal brands are the hallmark of helpful people. Once you've decided who your personal brand is most relevant to, go out of your way to be helpful to that audience. That might mean curating relevant industry information on your Twitter or LinkedIn feed. That might mean sending interesting articles to individuals by e-mail. That might mean blogging about issues of the day and how they impact your audience's business or outlook. Do what's manageable, but do something every week.

It's not surprising that Millennials are the first generation to fully grasp and implement the concept of personal branding. The evolution of the "Net" and social media has created an incredibly easy means for people from all walks of life to create powerful, influential personal brands, and today that branding expertise carries to the companies they will work for—either as free agents or contractors or employees.

In the same way that the logos we buy and the grocery brands we eat say something about us, the organization we work for and the work we do tell a story about who we are. Jobs and employers are part of people's identities, and in an environment when most people expect to have between eight and fifteen employers over the course of a career[2]—instead of just one to three—those jobs become as important to people in representing themselves as the clothes they wear, the bikes they ride, the food they eat, and the wine they drink.

In this context, the very common question from younger adults to recruiters—"Why should I work here?"—is natural, not the offensive, entitled question many older managers and recruiters have heard. The asker wants to know "What will it mean that I choose to work here? How will I make a difference? What will it convey to my friends and the world that I spend my time dedicated to this work?" So, if you are taken aback by questions you think inconceivable to have asked when you were looking for work, take a deep breath and resist the urge to write this candidate off. Most likely, she is probing to find the best fit for the way she sees herself.

## Responding to the New Interviewee Questions

| Question | Redirect before answering |
|---|---|
| Why should I work here? | Talk to me about what matters to you about the place you work. |
| What will this job set me up for? | Let me share with you some of the career paths of other people who have worked in this position. |
| Will I get promoted in less than a year? | What are your expectations and goals for this job? |
| How will I make a difference in this job? | How do you want to contribute? |
| How many volunteer days do I get in this job? | What are your philanthropic interests? (If your company doesn't have a way to contribute to the community, find one now.) |

Some companies have fully embraced this mind-set and have dedicated easy-to-find web pages to answer the question "Why should I work here?"

## The Talent Brand

This strong evolution of the importance of personal branding ironically has driven the recent emergence of the corporate talent brand. As much as companies need to create brands that attract and compel consumers and customers to purchase their products and services, they need to create brands for which talented employees and contractors will actively want to work.

In order to succeed in this staffing mindset, organizations need to create an identifiable value attribute hierarchy that matches the structure of personal brand attributes that today's employees have or are developing as seen in figure 3.1.

A talent brand is the sum of what current and former employees—the talent—feel, say, and share publicly about their employers. Strong talent brands attract employees with strong personal brands that highly align with their corporate brand attributes. From an employee's point of view, imagine a large overlap between a company's talent brand—vision,

| Talent Brand | Personal Brand |
|---|---|
| Vision | Purpose |
| Culture of Value | Respected & Respectful |
| Honors Past Contributions | Proud of Affiliations |
| High-Quality Work | High-Quality Work |

**Figure 3.1** Talent Brand–Personal Brand Value Hierarchy

# Talent Brand          Personal Brand

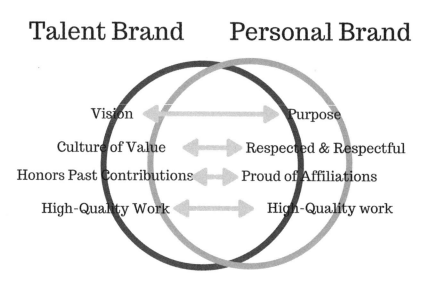

Vision ←→ Purpose

Culture of Value ←→ Respected & Respectful

Honors Past Contributions ←→ Proud of Affiliations

High-Quality Work ←→ High-Quality work

**Figure 3.2** Talent Brand–Personal Brand Alignment

values, culture, the way the company honors its former employees, opportunity, quality of work, industry position—and the employee's personal brand—personal mission or purpose, personal respect and collegiality, lifelong learning, strong work, values being associated with organizations.

From the company's perspective, imagine its talent brand overlapping with many different people. When people find companies that provide as much crossover or alignment with their brands as possible, and when companies find as many people as possible who have strong personal brands that align with their talent brand, the relationship between employer and employee succeeds. And mutually beneficial relationships between a company and its employees result in a healthy organization that generates positive business results. It's not rocket science, but it is a highly prized art form.

The Boomerang Principle—the belief that companies that allow and encourage former employees to return have a strategic advantage over those that don't—is all about the symbiotic relationship between healthy, sustainable businesses and the people (the talent) that propels them. It's all about the people and the power that people have to influence business success. If your company isn't a talent brand it can't be a boomerang brand either.

**Figure 3.3** Talent Brands Are The Sum of Their Employees' Personal Brands

Your employees have incredible power over your success not only when they are working and with the quality of their work but also with what they say to their friends and family about their work and their work experience. They can influence your success with what they share on social media—Instagram, LinkedIn, Facebook, Twitter, Snapchat, and so on—while they work for you. Whether they recommend the company when there are open positions and who they recommend is powerful and telling. Look to the way your people represent you out in the world—virtual and physical—and what they say about you when they leave your company.

With the highly public nature of branding—advertising, social media, reporting, sponsorship, and so on—talent brands create halos for corporate and product branding with more power than the reverse. If employees are the first audience for product success, they are the drivers of a company's success in recruiting and retaining the best employees.

As much as negative comments create speedbumps toward success, positive feelings help create the path of least resistance in reaching corporate goals. Even in down economies, when jobs are outnumbered by the qualified people who want them, negative sentiment hurts sustainability. That is exponentially true in sectors that demand more qualified people than exist.

More than 75 percent of job seekers consider a company's brand before they consider applying to a position. And 63 percent of all job seekers look at the various social media platforms to see what is being generated by and about an employer during the application process.[3] While the first place potential employees go when considering a position is the company's website, the second is social media platforms. Unsurprisingly, according to LinkedIn, LinkedIn ranks first among all of the social networks for this purpose. The third-ranking category of online destinations that job applicants use is job review sites, although 82 percent of job seekers visit these sites sometime in the process.[4]

Glassdoor and Career Bliss—two popular job and recruiting platforms that allow reviews from employees—have become a first stop for job recruits who want to get a handle on what it's like to work at the company. I have looked at hundreds of company reviews on these sites and, as with social networks, the veracity and the applicability of the content swings wildly. Frankly, the reviews on these sites are all over the map for most companies, ranging from very positive to very negative, from balanced and realistic to immature and whiny, and from glowing to glaring. Of course, the tenor of the reviews is dependent on who bothers to sign up and write a review—current or former, happy or disgruntled, fired or laid off, promoted or passed by. If you track the dates comments are posted, it's easy to imagine that employees were encouraged to share their positive experiences on a specific date. (Full disclosure: My company tracks and provides counsel for many of our clients regarding reviews on these sites as part of our work.) So while the information may or may not be relevant to any one applicant, it has become increasingly important in recruiting and management.

At the very least, companies should monitor sites such as Glassdoor and Career Bliss—as well as other social media channels—so they know what their potential employees are seeing and can be ready to address any questions that come up in interviews. Recommendations to improve overall scores on these sites range broadly depending on who's dispensing the advice. As with overall brand awareness programs, no one strategy fits all situations, and responses to the information you find should be tailored as the situation demands:

- Ensure that postings are within the site's guidelines for profanity, libel, and content. If a post violates the site's guidelines, contact the site to have it taken down or amended by the poster.
- If you know who posted a negative review, do not try to discredit that person on that site, in social media, or by other means. Consider reaching out to the former employee if you feel the posting reveals something you weren't aware of, in the spirit of learning from his experience. If the person agrees to meet with you, go to listen; do not ask him to remove the post. End the encounter in as positive a way as possible, wishing the former employee well.
- My company has counseled several companies about negative Glassdoor reviews that have revealed illegal activity by the poster or her colleagues. In these situations, it's critical to document the posts and take the high road; seek legal counsel quickly.
- If you know a current employee who has posted a negative review, help that person seek assistance in the company. Are you the manager? Meet with that person soon to explore what is wrong, what is fixable, and what steps you and she can take to improve the situation. Do not refer to the posting; instead, indicate that you are concerned that she is unhappy in her position. Do not ask her to remove the post. Fix what you can fix. (See chapter 6 for more.)

In the end, social networks are incredibly powerful tools for companies and employees, both happy and disgruntled, and they need to be monitored and managed. Internet trolls are easily identified by rational people—in my experience, there is virtually nothing you can do to stop trolls from trolling. The key thing is to make sure that the company is sharing positive, representative content on its own website and in social channels.

In the next chapters I will show you how to create exceptional talent brands—they aren't just for the big guys. Every company of two or more people needs to be a talent brand that attracts and retains strong, talented employees who have strong personal brands. If you have a compelling talent brand, you are halfway to realizing the full effect of the Boomerang Principle.

# CHAPTER 4

# Creating a Culture of Return
# Creates a Culture to Stay For

The key to having people return to your company is being a place people want to return to. The irony, of course, is that the more effort you devote to creating a culture that welcomes people back, the better the culture is for the people who are in your organization today. Focusing effort on making the current organization the best it can be will pay dividends this year and next; *not* putting effort into training your people out of fear of them leaving will push them out the door faster.

It all comes down to culture. "Nothing is more important than culture," says Rob Castaneda, president and CEO of ServiceRocket, a fifteen-year-old software company that has many boomerang employees, clients, and partners. "As we've built out the company from Sydney to Palo Alto, Kuala Lumpur, and now Santiago, Chile, we have focused on bringing our work culture to each office and making them definitively 'ServiceRocket' but also relevant in each location," Castaneda says. "It's incredibly time consuming, but it's paid off over and over again as we've grown and pivoted to our position." Service Rocket has more than a dozen people who have returned to the company, as well as another dozen or so who have become clients or partners.

A Boomerang culture is a culture of *value* (see Figure 4.1).

# A Boomerang Culture Is a Culture of Value

## Vision & Values
## Appreciation
## Leadership
## OpportUnity & Possibility
## Expectations

**Figure 4.1** Culture of Value Hierarchy

## A Culture of Vision and Values

The evolution of the purpose-driven life in American culture has dramatically altered what people look for in their work and careers. While Boomers, and to a lesser extent Gen Xers, may have worked their way up the ladder and had personal lives they kept separate from their work lives, Millennials are generally focused on finding or creating work that aligns with their purpose in life. "Why would I spend more than one hour a day on something that doesn't match my purpose?" said one Millennial I spoke with. "There's only so many days we each have, and I want to make sure I don't regret any of them."

This was part of a wide-ranging conversation with a twenty-nine-year-old senior product manager in Buffalo, New York. Throughout this conversation, and in the more than one hundred interviews and three thousand surveys of Millennials across the country, it became very clear that finding work with a company that has a clearly stated vision—and values that back it up—that aligns with personal purpose is a high priority for many of the almost eighty million Millennials in the United States, more than twenty million of whom haven't yet left school.

To attract talent that can propel them forward, organizations need to be able to provide clear paths so that their individual employees can readily see how each of their roles and purpose in the organization ties

**Figure 4.2**  Corporate Vision to Individual Purpose: A Direct Link

to the overall vision of the company. I recommend using chart like this one so that managers can clearly show how each person contributes to the company's business.

## Vision and Mission

Vision and mission statements are often confused with each other or are interchanged, but they are distinctive, though related. Vision and mission statements are two critical organizing principles for any company, of any size, in any industry, and at any stage. They are the key ingredients of your company's special sauce.

Vision: the imprint you want to make in the world
Mission: what you do every day to bring your vision closer to
   reality

In general, the company vision—the imprint you want to make in the world or the positive state of the future world you imagine in your industry—stays relatively constant over time. Great visions are based in the future; they are aspirational and big; they are emotionally charged and paint a positive or hopeful picture of the future. A vision statement should be short and use clear language. A company's vision may or may not be outwardly facing, yet everyone in the company should know and be able to say and share it.

The company mission should roll off the tongue just as easily as the vision statement, and it is definitively outward facing. Mission statements are based in the present and encapsulate what the company does—and therefore what every person does—every day to bring the company vision closer to reality. Good mission statements are achievement oriented and articulate the essential purpose of the company. They should be short—one to two sentences—and use clear and compelling active language. No one should react to a mission statement with "What does that mean?" Instead, they should know that the mission is why we do what we do. In the best of all worlds, it's why we get out of bed in the morning.

Everyone in a company should be able to say and share its vision and mission. You should share your vision widely in recruiting cycles so everyone your company talks with understands the organizing principle for the company's mission and purpose.

If you search for vision statements, you may not find them on company websites because these statements often paint a hopeful picture of the future that may seem unattainable—they are best used as internal rallying cries and organizing principles. Mission statements, on the other hand, should be easy to find and easy to read for your employees, customers, partners, communities, prospects, and, yes, your former employees. Today, brands that don't stand for anything that people can grab on to don't stand a chance over the long haul.

A culture of vision and values starts with an inspiring picture of the future and a purpose-filled mission that tells everyone listening why your employees get up in the morning to come to work.

Following are some good examples of statements from companies and organizations you may or may not know:

## Ikea

Vision: Our vision is to create a better everyday life for many people.

Mission: To offer a wide range of well-designed functional home furnishing products at prices so low that as many people as possible can afford them.

## Microsoft

Vision: Make a difference in lives and organizations in all corners of the planet.

Mission: To empower every person and every organization on the planet to achieve more.

## National Multiple Sclerosis Association

Vision: A world free of MS.

Mission: Stop MS in its tracks, restore what has been lost, and end MS forever.

## Jet Blue

Vision: To better the lives of our customers, our crewmembers, and the communities we serve.

Mission: To inspire humanity both in the air and on the ground.

## The Marine Mammal Center

Vision: A healthy ocean for marine mammal and humans alike.

Mission: To advance global ocean conservation through marine mammal rescue and rehabilitation, scientific research, and education.

Mission statements without vision statements can stand on their own for people outside the organization as long as they are aspirational and differentiate the organization or company from others operating in the same sphere.

**Cradles to Crayons**

Mission: To provide children from birth to age twelve, living in homeless or low-income situations, with the essential items they need to thrive—at home, at school, and at play.

**Patagonia**

Mission: Build the best product, cause no unnecessary harm, use business to inspire, and implement solutions to the environmental crisis.

**Navitas Naturals**

Mission: The mission of Navitas Naturals is to provide the finest organic superfoods that increase energy and enhance health.

Without a compelling vision—your company's hope for the world—and its related mission—what your company does every day to bring that hope closer to reality—your company will lack the glue that keeps people in place and pulling in the same direction.

*Values*

The values of an organization—the guiding principles that define individual and group behavior and standards—are equally important to the company's vision and mission in the eyes of today's workforce. In assessing the data in the 2016 Deloitte Millennial Survey, the consulting firm declares that "values guide where Millennials work, what assignments they will accept."[1] In fact, among almost 7,700 respondents, 70 percent, believe "their personal values are shared by the organizations they work for" and 56 percent have "ruled out ever working for a particular organization because of its values or standard of conduct."[2]

Jim Collins and Jerry Porras highlighted the importance to sustainable companies of a shared language and clear understanding of behaviors and principles in their best-selling book, *Built to Last*. Collins and Porras's research showed that the companies that withstood the test of time all had their own sets of principles or values that "preserv[ed] the essence of the organization" over time.[3]

As Patrick Lencioni describes in his book *The Advantage: Why Organizational Health Trumps Everything Else in Business*, "The importance of values in creating clarity and enabling a company to become healthy cannot be overstated."[4] And it's not just values in theory, but overt values-based behavior standards that are usually understood, met, and aspirational.

Too often, though, values are lists of aspirational words on a page left up to interpretation. As time goes by, they wither on the vine either because the group has forgotten what they mean or because the interpretation of the words varies with each person who reads them. How often have you seen the words *integrity, teamwork, humility, growth, communication,* or *empowerment* on the list of values? Yet when you walk around different companies using the same words, they feel and perform very differently. When is the last time you asked your team what your corporate values are? Can they roll the words off their tongues without looking at the wall or their mugs?

Words are not enough to create a foundation of behavior that binds people together. Values that work help people refuse to tolerate bad behavior in the workplace. As Lencioni says, "If an organization is tolerant of everything, it will stand for nothing."[5] Instead of just leaving the words on the page, companies must articulate—in clear, easily repeatable language—what those words mean for the company. In *The Advantage,* Lencioni lays out an easy-to-follow system to help teams identify the values that matter to them, breaking values down into the categories "core," "permission to play," "aspirational," and "accidental."

At Double Forte, we revamped our values in 2015, adapting Lencioni's model to our situation, when I realized that our longer-tenured and shorter-tenured employees had different definitions of some of the words on our wall. Our process was an all-company effort, and it involved getting input from everyone and then honing in on the core values, what we call *bedrock*, and adding others that are aspirational.

Double Forte's values are:

- We are a team
- Growth matters
- We answer the call
- We get sh*t done—well
- We are a force for good
- We take care of our own
- We are fiercely courageous
- We strive to be the SEAL Team Six of our industry

These may look weird or mundane, depending on your point of view. However, generating this list was just part of the exercise. Step two was to articulate exactly what we mean when we say these words, in terms of behaviors, actions, attitudes, and priorities.

What makes our values different is the way we define them. For example:

**Growth matters**

Our team members:
- Know work can be improved and **seek** to have it improved by colleagues
- Are **receptive** to new ideas about how to approach work, outcomes, process, etc.
- Appreciate that everyone has his own definition of "growth," contributes to the team, and is on **his own** career path
- **Take** responsibility for their own development plan

**We answer the call**

We:
- Get to "no" through "yes"
- Have a "what can I do for you" attitude with colleagues, clients, partners, and others

- Do not add to client or colleague workload; we always produce pass-along-able work
- Demonstrate appropriate sense of urgency to team, clients, partners, and others
- Do not overpromise and under deliver
- Are able to flex and cater to different client work and communications styles/needs
- Communicate to stop it—efficiently communicate to drive clarity with clients, colleagues, partners, and others

**We get sh\*t done—well**

Our team members:

- Are accountable for their work, words, and actions
- Do not leave people hanging—if a team member says it, she does it on time, to the best of her ability
- Solve problems first and then figure out how to avoid them in the future
- Demonstrate willingness to do excellent work through results, thoroughness, timeliness
- Learn from trial and error; do not repeat mistakes

**We are fiercely courageous**

Our team:

- Is not easily defeated
- Makes hard decisions
- Contributes contrary ideas in a constructive manner to improve work or company
- Looks for the best solution, even if it's wacky or staid or doesn't benefit the company's bottom line

We have more examples of the way we elaborate our values, but those mentioned illustrate the point. The more specificity you can put around the words, the clearer you can be about which behaviors are in and which are out of alignment with your values.

we are a team • growth matters • answer the call • we get sh*t done well • we are good people • we take care of our own • fun-loving • force for good • fiercely courageous • special ops of our industry

**Figure 4.3**  Double Forte Values & Hero Image

Sharing your values during the recruiting process will help you sift out people who don't want to operate in alignment with your values. This doesn't make them bad people; it just makes them people who don't belong in your organization.

We've had a few people we were hoping would join the firm review our values and tap out of the recruiting process altogether. One person over forty—a very qualified professional I had worked with before—wasn't keen on having everyone weigh in on his work or on the possibility of having to change the way he'd done things his whole career. He asked me, "Is this for everyone or just for the inexperienced people?" "It's for everyone," I answered. He replied, "I don't think this is the place for me." I wished him well.

On the other hand, sharing our values has been the thing that tipped a few highly sought-after candidates in our favor. One woman read the values and stared at me for a few moments before exclaiming "This is me!" She started a week later.

A culture of vision and values is one with an easily identified purpose and a commonly held understanding of behaviors and standards everyone can hold up. Companies that have a clear and compelling vision and values not only attract great talent more easily, but they also avoid hiring as many people who are ill-suited for their cultures and they shed people who are out of alignment more quickly.

## A Culture of Appreciation

Millennials get dinged for being a generation of trophy lovers and for needing constant praise. Well, it's not their fault that their parents foisted ribbons, pins, trophies, and certificates on them for every activity . . . all the way through college. I think everyone-wins soccer is great too—until first grade. And if we think the kids don't actually know who scored more runs or goals, we are fooling ourselves.

> The best baseball game to watch in the world is a Challenger game between two teams made up of developmentally or physically handicapped kids. Each inning is however long it takes for everyone to bat, and there are no outs. Each game has four inside-the-park grand slams, and parents and other spectators are cheering for every kid as they amble, roll, stumble, run, or walk around the bases. My younger son plays Challenger baseball, and it is a joy to watch him drop to his knees three-quarters of the way from third base and then "slide" his way into home plate, pulling himself with his arms stretched out.

When I say "a culture of appreciation," I'm talking about a culture in which effort and achievement are actively acknowledged by everyone. As I've said previously, "Gratuitous appreciation has no place in the workplace."[6] I came to this understanding in 2011 when my company started hiring Millennials. While I grew up understanding that I should use *please* and *thank you* in social situations, it wasn't clear to me that these words belonged in the workplace. Growing up, I had worked in my father's labs for several summers, where I assisted in his cardiac research operating on dogs and pigs. There was no time for please and thank you during the procedures—only at the end of the operation would the lead say "Thanks, team." And my first several jobs did not have cultures of appreciation either. I'm a nice person (so they tell me), and it was crushing to hear "Why don't you ever say thank you to us, Lee?" from a frustrated younger colleague. While I never thought that a paycheck was a thank you, it was hard to hear that some people thought I didn't appreciate them.

So I started saying please and thank you all the time. At first I felt ridiculous, like everyone was going to think I was making fun of my colleagues. But after a week, it came more naturally, and after a month, please and thank you and their alternatives permeated my conversations.

Teams who feel appreciated outperform those who don't.
—Lori Ogden Moore, executive coach

Adding niceties to my conversations with staff made a big difference—for me and for the people around me. I'm here to tell you that the more we say please and thank you, the better our organizations will be.

Indeed, as researchers Francesca Gino of Harvard and Adam Grant of Wharton concluded, most of us "don't realize how powerful it is to say thank you . . . and the effects are large. And they're important."[7]

The better people feel about their contributions, the better the morale of the group, which contributes to a positive work environment, which, in turn, improves performance and increases talent longevity. And it's not only the receiver of the appreciation who benefits. Gino explains the results of many studies that show that the bestowers of thanks "experience all sorts of positive emotions. They're more attentive, alert, energetic, feel, again, happy about life in general."[8]

Different companies have different ways, beyond please and thank you, to show appreciation, from bonuses to trophies to shout-outs to flowers. Personally, I find that, next to please and thank you, the best way to show your appreciation for someone's efforts is by sharing your appreciation with other people. My best days are those when I get an e-mail from someone in my company, or from a client or partner, bringing her appreciation for someone's work, attitude, or contribution to my attention. One, it means a lot that a person took a moment to write the e-mail; two, it demonstrates that the sender gets the "team" thing; three, now I can pile on and add my thanks to the person as well.

## A Culture of Leadership

The standard coaching line is "people leave managers, they don't leave companies." I'm not so sure. Actually, I am sure. Companies that allow bad managers to flourish are responsible for good people leaving because of those managers. And in today's world, where every company is its own talent brand, bad managers and leaders are more of a liability than ever.

Leadership development is the new black.

Leaders provide direction, make decisions, and solve problems. Leadership is not the sole purview of those with seniority or rank. In our fast-moving, increasingly interdependent business environment, every company needs leaders at every level and in every seat.

Millennials are used to moving in and out of leadership positions or responsibility often, and they expect to lead in their work. Put another way, Millennials believe they can lead from any seat in the boat and that they have it in them to lead at any moment. Lack of leadership development is a key driver of Millennials' job dissatisfaction, and Millennials who are actively considering leaving their current positions within twelve to twenty-four months are significantly more likely to say that they are "being overlooked for potential leadership positions" or that their "leadership skills are not being developed."

Modern leadership—what has evolved in the last twenty years and features concepts including servant leadership, emotional intelligence, failing forward, and so on—is the antithesis of the command-and-control, do-it-because-I- told-you-to, and don't-show-any-vulnerability leadership models of the past. While Boomers, the "wait my turn generation," may have been comfortable with hierarchy and Gen Xers may have been confident in their abilities to make things happen without a lot of input, Millennials demand a new style of leadership that encompasses an increasingly dynamic and geographically dispersed workforce and business opportunities.

We all need leaders at every level in our organizations.

And while the oldest Millennials entered the leadership ranks in the last four or five years, they feel less prepared than they want to for the role. Seventy-two percent of the Millennials I surveyed (all in the U.S.) are unhappy with the training provided to prepare them for the leadership roles they are coming into. This is echoed by Deloitte's international survey of Millennials, 63 percent of whom indicated that their "leadership skills are not being fully developed."[9] And this dissatisfaction in leadership development correlates directly with these employees' likeliness to leave their positions "in the next two years."

"We are dying out here because no one knows how to inspire people to action," shared one twenty-eight-year-old respondent from Chicago. Another respondent said, "I keep being asked to do more, to take on more large projects, but they've just thrown it into my lap without helping me understand how to get to the next level." When I shared this type of feedback with a panel of senior executives, their responses ranged from rolling of the eyes to heavy sighs and statements like "Where's their initiative?! No one told me how to lead, and I've been doing it for over ten years."

Millennials are the most "instructed" generation in American history today. More Millennials per capita, and therefore by raw number, have earned bachelor's degrees or their equivalent, and the sixteen- to twenty-year-old cohort hasn't yet graduated—that number is only going up. They are used to having "a class for that" and being shown where to get the information they need to succeed. It doesn't much matter what we did in the past that did or did not work. The point is that leadership development is a capacity-building exercise for your organization. Leadership is hard, and to expect anyone to just "know how" without ample training and support is a false assumption. This has always been true. The difference is that Millennials expect leadership training regardless of their position in an organization.

Moving from a role as an individual contributor taking care of himself to a position of manager responsible for other people's performance has always been challenging. Learning to lead has never been more challenging. Roughly two million people are promoted into leadership positions each year, and 60 percent of them fail in some way—that's 1.2 million failures for first-time leaders.[10] The irony is not lost here—almost $14 billion is dedicated to leadership development programs every year,[11] and yet the return on that investment is terrible given the failure rate.

So we can either keep doing what we've been doing and keep getting these results, or we can break out from the statistics and show our people how to lead in our organizations by mentoring, coaching, and developing them instead of training them against a standard. I pick option two: It's cheaper, it helps deliver the results we need, and it's an investment that will pay dividends in affinity and goodwill long after that person has left us. And my head doesn't hurt anymore since I've stopped banging it against the wall.

## Different Ways to Approach Leadership Development

The most important role of a leader is to develop leadership throughout the organization—for high performers and not-so-high performers, for individual contributors who will never manage other people, and for managers of people and projects alike. You never know when someone will need to lead from the fourth seat of an eight-man boat. Following are some resources you can use to help employees at all levels of your organization develop leadership skills:

- **Leadership development courses and curricula.** Such courses are abundant, and their quality is as wide ranging as the offerings. If you're going to go down this route, know that the "trainee" will need ample coaching and mentoring to be able to apply what is taught in the classes.
- **A reading list.** Curate a list of leadership books that will create a knowledge base for your organization, and provide the books for everyone. Having people read the same books is incredibly effective at reinforcing shared values and behavior expectations. Bill Gates's blog *gatesnotes* is an excellent source of inspiration for reading lists. Consider the following:
  - *Superbosses: How Exceptional Leaders Master the Flow of Talent* by Sydney Finkelstein
  - *The Advantage: Why Organizational Health Trumps Everything Else in Business* by Patrick Lencioni
  - *Primal Leadership: Learning to Lead with Emotional Intelligence* by Daniel Goleman, Richard Boyatzis, and Annie McKee
  - *Drive* by Daniel H. Pink
  - *The Alchemist* by Paulo Coelho
  - *The Truth about Leadership* by James M. Kouzes and Barry Z. Posner
  - *Tribes: We Need You to Lead Us* by Seth Godin
  - *Team of Rivals* by Doris Kearns Goodwin

## The Emergence of Coaching

Executive or leadership coaching can be incredibly powerful and transformative for employees at all levels and classifications, from contributor to manager to leader. And, increasingly, Millennials don't want "managers," they want coaches or people who act as stewards of their positions and careers; developing a strong coaching style is critical if you want to foster both overall organizational health and positive momentum on your teams.

Coaching is becoming increasingly accessible to employees, first, because the universe of qualified coaches has exploded in the last decade and, second, because new online platforms are providing ad hoc and ongoing coaching services at affordable prices for individuals and organizations.

Some of the organizations providing coaching via online platforms include the following:

- BetterUp: www.betterup.co—online performance coaching platform for the enterprise
- ICF: www.coachfederation.org—the International Coaching Federation, the largest organization of professionally trained coaches
- The Muse: www.themuse.com—online career resource offering executive coaching services for new managers

If your company is not able or ready to offer company-wide coaching options, consider offering coaching "allowances" as part of the total benefit package. The responsibility moves to the employee to find a reputable, legitimate coach best suited to match their personality and needs that meets the company's criteria for reimbursement - however strict. Price points and formats vary greatly, from intense week-long retreats to group online sessions and apps that "gamify" goal-setting and achievement. Some effective options include:

- Happy at Work online coaching www.havenecarter.com
- Waveworkscoaching.com career coaching
- Remente mobile app
- SuccessWiz mobile app

A culture of leadership builds capacity throughout the organization and develops individuals' abilities to maneuver, contribute meaningfully, and solve problems before they escalate. Companies with a culture of leadership have significantly more capacity than those that concentrate leadership in the hands of a few senior executives.

## A Culture of Opportunity and Possibility

When employees expect to move from place to place or position to position to build their own careers, keeping good talent with your company depends significantly on how much opportunity each employee feels he has to progress toward his individual goals.

In my first book, I shared a story from Ted, then a forty-seven-year-old general manager at one of the largest software companies in the world. He had a high-performing woman on his team in her late twenties who said to him, "You know and I know that I'm not going to be here forever, so what's the next best thing I can do here? Help me figure this out so I can have a great experience before I'm done."[12] Ted took a week to think about it, realizing that she had said out loud what everyone else was probably thinking. The next time they met, he mapped out a twelve- to eighteen-month plan via which this employee could be "valuable to the team and get value for herself" with some expanded roles and responsibilities. Ted made it clear that he expected "100 percent participation during this time." She was happy and he had gotten a commitment from her. He ended that story with "I hope it works out."

I talked to Ted again in researching this book, and he shared that the woman was still there three years later. "She did a great job in the first path we created, and we created another one together for the next twelve to eighteen months, which she is about halfway through." This experience provided great learning for Ted. He met with all of his direct reports "off cycle" to have candid conversations about each of those people's goals, and with each of them mapped out twelve- to twenty-four-month paths with clear performance expectations and responsibilities. "Everyone had his or her own plan, and the great thing is that I knew what they were—beyond just getting the work done—so I was able to coach along the way. And my team had its best performance ever once we had those plans in place." Ted shared that all of his people "put in extra" to help make their plans work, a pattern I've seen over and over again in my own career.

The power of opportunity and possibility to attract and then retain great people is compelling. I've gotten over the shock of hearing "Why should I work here?" in interviews; I know it's what is on young people's minds, and they haven't had enough experience to know how to ask the question with more finesse. Now, I focus on what people think they want to do, what they need to learn, and whether they can accomplish that given the construct of the company's business and future plans.

What are the opportunities at your workplace for other people? Be prepared to articulate a wide range of possibilities that are dependent on employees making it work. And then be prepared to work with each person to create a path that leads toward her goals in a way that doesn't compromise the business or the team. This is critical. If everyone has the same opportunity to achieve their goals and does their jobs at the same time, it works. It's when there's a perception—or the reality—that someone is getting special attention and isn't pulling her weight that resentment creeps in. Possibility and opportunity need to be universal within the confines of the work at hand.

Here are just a few of the questions and statements we've heard that we put in our "Opportunity and Possibility File":

- Can I work from home with my own schedule?
- My father is ill. I'd like a schedule that lets me go to doctor appointments with him.
- I'd like to be able to coach a kids' soccer team for twelve weeks a year.
- I want to be a vice president before I'm thirty.

- My background is all technology, but I really want to work on wine accounts. Can I do that?
- I'm interested in learning from you how to start my own company.
- I'm a performer. Can we create a schedule that gets my work done in time for me to get to rehearsals and performances?
- I've only been an individual contributor. I want to be a manager with several people under me. How will you teach me how to do that?
- I'm training for a marathon and my schedule is pretty rigid. I'd like to make sure I don't have to compromise my training schedule to work here.
- I want to go into an entirely different career, but I think the skills I'd learn here would really help me. Is that okay?

For the Boomers in the crowd, can you even imagine asking these questions in an interview for an entry- or junior-level job? I know many of you can't; I hear from incredulous older workers all the time about this issue. Get over it. Everything is possible if you have a culture of high expectations and ownership.

## A Culture of Expectations

For many people this culture of value—vision and values, appreciation, leadership, and opportunity and possibility—seems coddling and accommodating. It's not, as long your team also has a culture of high expectations and ownership.

Expectations only work if you say them out loud.

None of these other principles works unless the business is achieving its goals in revenue and profit; there is no business without a business.

Your team must have a common understanding of the expectations for behavior (expressed in your values), performance, and business targets, as well as an understanding of the consequences if expectations are not met. At the same time, with today's disparate work schedules, employees need to take personal responsibility for owning their work product and their behavior. People who don't own their behavior or their work need to prove they can before accommodations are made.

You can't communicate these expectations often enough. Said differently: Do not assume that everyone understands and remembers expectations unless they are constantly reinforced. In marketing, we used to use the numbers seven or twelve—the number of times the right person had to see the message to make it stick. Today, we use much higher numbers, ranging from twenty-four to thirty-six. There is little white space left in our day where messaging and advertising aren't in our sightline, and to get through to the target audience, repetition requirements are much higher.

I'm not suggesting that you need to send an e-mail twenty-four times before it will be heard. I am suggesting that everyone on your team needs to regularly reinforce the agreed-upon expectations among the group in order to drive performance and collaboration. Do this in e-mail, at the start of meetings, and before you give feedback. Reinforce, reinforce, reinforce . . . did I say reinforce? Repetition is your friend.

Expectations should be shared during the recruiting process so there are no surprises when people show up on their first day. My rule of thumb is that "everything is possible if you make it work for your team and your client." My expectation is that people prioritize the team over themselves in making their requests work. For example, if a team member has a rigid training schedule, she needs to (1) let the team know what it is, (2) move her work around so that no one is waiting for her to do her job when she's out training, (3) know that there may be situations that require her attendance during training hours, and (4) understand that if she doesn't do these things, she loses the privilege.

In my experience, people meet expectations when they know what the expectations are. A culture of high expectations around performance, behavior, teamwork, and communication, along with shared ownership, ensures clarity, efficiency, and performance so that everyone is pulling in the same direction together, even if their oars look different and enter the water at different times.

A culture worth returning to is a culture worth staying for. At the same time, not every company will be able to "hold" every one of its prized employees' aspirations. Don't worry about that. Worry about the culture people are working in now—if it's good, the future will take care of itself.

# CHAPTER 5

# When Millennials Thrive, So Do Gen Xers and Boomers

The irony in the surprise or disgruntlement we feel when employees move on is, of course, that when we hire people, we know they are going to leave us. And yet when they do, we often act surprised and affronted: "How can you do this?" "Where's the loyalty?" "We've done so much for you." Really, only one person needs to be there to turn the lights out, and it probably wouldn't have been that employee anyway. Heck, unless you're the owner, it's probably not you either.

Millennials, particularly in the first years after they graduate from college, start jobs and expect that they won't stay past five years—and sometimes only two or three years. They've got lots of anecdotal stories and advice around them reinforcing this thought—friends who've job-hopped looking for that great situation, parents who've counseled them not to stay too long if there isn't rapid advancement lest they look stale. And, of course, most recent graduates know the world through three- or four-year increments of time: middle school, high school, and college.

Add to this the shock of entering the job market. High expectations collide with the reality of the workplace, and too often disillusion sets in. Entry-level jobs, incommensurate with what many college graduates believe they are qualified to do, can be disheartening if they are not overtly valued by the organization and understood in the context of a longer opportunity. If strong company leadership isn't in place from day one to help guide and mentor new hires through onboarding, and if Millennials feel that they aren't listened to or can't contribute as they wish, then on to the next job they go.

## One Millennial's Story

Amy, a twenty-four-year-old graduate of Northwestern University who has a good position managing social media presence for a prestigious organization, shared a point of view that perfectly sums up the many interviews I conducted with recent college graduates who'd started working:

> There's so much effort put into landing a job when you're in college. Internships, resume-building, interviews—the pressure is heavy to land a job as fast as you can so you can start paying off your student debt. But no one talks about what it's like to actually work the job you get—and it's been a shock for me and most of my friends.
>
> In each of my four internships at four different companies in three different cities, which are so important to getting a job, there was a lot of effort made to help me understand the projects I had to do. Each one I was assigned to, someone was responsible for making sure I got out of the internship what I was supposed to for the credit I was getting at school. My college internship coordinator was very proud of the work they do to vet each internship for credit to make sure we aren't just getting coffee or running errands for people. But the internship experience is far different from the actual job it leads to.
>
> The biggest shocks for me were how independent my forty-year-old manager expected me to be, how challenging it would be to get what I needed to know to do my job well out of my manager, and how irritated people who'd been there

for a while would be when I asked questions. Sitting in the same space all day was a big adjustment too.

And then there's this whole workplace etiquette thing. I grew up and went to college in the Midwest—the manner rules seem to be much different in New York than in Chicago. Add to that all the unspoken rules in my office—don't be the first person to rush to the kitchen if there's food, don't wear earbuds at work until after twelve, don't use texting after hours, and so on.

I think we all learn fast that our first jobs aren't "the job"— but all my friends and I talk about how much we wish someone would have spent at least a little time on the realities of work while they were preparing us to get work.

Nearly 80 percent of college students think they are above average, according to the American Freshman Survey produced annually by the Cooperative Institutional Research Program at the Higher Education Research Institute at UCLA.[1] No wonder the reality of the "real world" crashes in as new graduates begin their working lives—and then Millennials end up leaving sooner than even they had planned.

Of course, Millennials aren't alone! "Everyone thinks they are above average," according to David Dunning of Cornell University. [2] In fact, illusory superiority "is so stubbornly persistent that psychologists would be surprised if it didn't show up in their studies," Dunning says. So stop pointing at just the Millennials!

Given the reality or even just the perception of job-hopping Millennials, many managers I've talked to have pulled back on training for everyone. "Why should I put the time into training these people? They're going to leave anyway and I'll just have to start over again." Thus starts a vicious cycle predetermined to create inefficiency and a downward spiral for any team. Managers pull back on their training and mentoring programs, leaving unsatisfied employees yearning and expecting mentoring and growth opportunities, which in turn creates manager dissatisfaction in the work product and output. This, in turn, leads to employees feeling that they "need to leave" for work environments more attuned to their career and life goals.

As I heard one professionally dressed young woman, who apparently had just left her job, say to her tablemate at a coffee shop in Boston, "I would rather help my mom out at home than sit in that soul-sucking job without a future where no one cares about me." In a world where more Millennials aged eighteen to thirty-four years live in their parents' homes than with a spouse or partner in their own households,[3] the parental safety net may seem like the best option for unhappy younger employees.

Of course, this negative dynamic isn't the sole province of entry-level jobs. Employees of all ages, at all levels, in all industries complain that the positions and opportunities they were promised or that they perceived during the recruiting process are not the ones they actually have. Older people may have an experience-based understanding that leaving without a new position often makes it harder to find the next job or that moving on before putting in a certain amount of time can "flag" a resume in the future. Or, frankly, older employees may feel that if they leave an unfulfilling job, they may be unable to find a new position at all. Ageism is alive and well across the country.

Many Boomers and Gen Xers have difficulty finding work commensurate with their experience or salary expectations in industries or regions that have been negatively impacted by the Great Recession. Companies moving work to "cheaper" cities or countries or implementing disruptive technology or business models have rendered those with once-prized skill sets unemployable in many places with large populations. This type of disruption is not new, of course—the agrarian, industrial, and first technology revolutions that led us to our current lifestyle are distant memories, but that doesn't make living through this seismic shift any easier for the people most negatively impacted.

Millennials and their younger siblings, Generation Z, have created—and are creating—a different dynamic at work because of the technology-based advantages they have been born into and what the huge shifts in the economy have meant to the workforce, and this has shaken up businesses big and small across the country. Millennials, like every generation before them, are leaving their imprint on the workplace. And they will continue to change the employment landscape, given that the youngest Millennials, in 2017, are at least six years from college-graduate age (twenty-two).

The difference between the workplace changes wrought by earlier generations and those brought by Millennials is that they affect a broader age range of working people: we are decades away from the oldest employees today—Boomers and Traditionalists—retiring from the workplace. Today, most businesses have three generations—Boomers, Gen Xers, and Millennials—working side by side, and many have four, with millions of people seventy-two and older still in the workplace, giving the working population an age range from sixteen to eighty-something.

## Differences of the Time

Although in general I eschew characterizing Millennials in a negative way, I have found several commonalities among them that, once understood, can help organizations create positive intergenerational work teams.

### Hierarchy Is Antithetical to the Millennial Experience

This is particularly true of younger Millennials, those sixteen to twenty-eight years old. Raised with a rationalized Internet literally in their hands, Millennials are used to having access to any information they want, the ability to contact any person they want through e-mail or social media, and the capacity to mobilize action and sentiment. (Of course, "anything they want" is hyperbole—search engines still only index a fraction of what is available on the Internet, and what they do index is never up to date.[4] But still the perception prevails.) It's not uncommon for Millennials at any level in an organization to expect senior executives at the highest level to not just grant, but look for, regular and meaningful interaction from everyone in the organization. For people who appreciate or expect a more hierarchical business structure, this flat-world expectation is challenging to accommodate and work with.

## Millennials Expect to Have Work That Matters

The purpose of the company, the team, and the position are critical factors for Millennials considering different positions. Organizations that "demonstrate a strong sense of purpose beyond financial success" are actively sought after as employers by Millennials.[5]

> I chose this job, even though I had a higher offer, because my company has two volunteer days a year we can take and has regular team-based volunteer activities throughout the year. I want to be in a place where I can make a difference at my work *and* through my work.
>
> —Julie, a twenty-five-year-old sales associate based in Minneapolis

To that point, Millennials expect to matter in their roles, regardless of where they sit in the position ladder. Pay particular attention to the most junior people on your teams, making sure that they understand how critical their work is to the rest of the team; I've found that this goes a very long way to reducing the frustration people have about working in what they consider "menial positions." It never hurts to remind someone who is unhappy that he's not doing something "more important"—that no one pays for work that doesn't have to get done.

Giving input that is valued and incorporated *is* the Millennial experience. Millennials expect that their input will be appreciated from the beginning of their careers. They have grown up with technology and connected devices that are unapologetically imperfect. They know to check for product and application updates regularly, and when they find a bug or a glitch—older people would have called them mistakes or flaws—they share their experiences with, and often are compensated by, the companies that distribute these products. This is radically different from the experience of previous generations, who bought games and software on discs, cartridges, or CDs and there was no way to improve them until the next version came out . . . on another disc or cartridge or CD.

Millennials' feedback and evaluations of college classes, professors, and instructors have had significant impact in their school careers. As one professor of humanities at a West Coast research university explained for the higher education publication *Chronicle Vitae*, the average student evaluation score that keeps nontenured professors "safe" at their universities is 4.7 on a five-point scale. The ranking dominates conversation in the department, with more time spent on "how we get into the 4.7 and above range" than about how to teach.[6] In this reality, it's no wonder Millennials feel a responsibility to point out flaws or make suggestions. The companies they've purchased from have benefitted from their feedback almost all their lives—why wouldn't it be the same at their jobs?

In the more than five hundred interviews I've done with Millennials in the past three years, I have heard one rendition or another of "Why don't they ask my opinion?" time and time again. As Eden, a twenty-six-year-old graphic designer shared with me, she left two jobs because her ideas weren't considered or even asked for. At one job, she said, "Every time I made a suggestion about how to get the work done I was told that I wasn't allowed to give input on how the team would work together. I left there fast."

Solicit input from your team before you start a project. While you are setting the context for a project or work stream, ask everyone to weigh in on how, together, the team might streamline the workflow, make a bigger impact, or rearrange the schedule. You may not be able to apply everyone's feedback; be sure to thank people for their ideas and explain why they might not be feasible this time.

The practice of soliciting authentically, considering, and applying input will create much more cohesive teams and much more clarity, and it will help everyone understand that they matter to the team.

## Millennials Have Come of Age Hearing
## Two Main Themes about Work

First, *work–life balance* has been a major theme in business reporting and discussion for more than twenty years—you don't need to be a rocket scientist to figure out that the children of the women (mostly) who beat the work–life balance drum relentlessly expect to receive what their parents worked hard for as soon as they enter the workplace. At the same time, with the pervasiveness of technology, many Millennials are quite adept at weaving together work responsibilities and life responsibilities and interests throughout the day. Therefore, work–life balance looks different for this younger generation. Whereas Boomers and Gen Xers may have worked regular hours and had a clear delineation between work and life, communication technology has rendered that divide negligible or imaginary.

The second thing Millennials have learned is: *Don't get stale.* Millennial children of Boomers and Xers who were impacted by the financial collapse of 2008–2009 and its aftermath are particularly sensitive to the risks of staying at one company or in one position for a long time. They do not expect or want to stay with one company for a long period, and they expect to change their career tracks several times over the course of their working years.

Sixty percent of Millennials age twenty-two to thirty-two have "changed jobs between one and four times in the last five years,"[7] 44 percent of Millennials "would leave their current employer in the next two years if given the choice," and 66 percent expect to have switched employers in the next four years.[8] In my own research, for Millennials, one to two years and two to four years were the most popular answers to the question "How long would you like to stay at your current job?" while Boomers almost unanimously chose five or more years.

## Millennials Want Leaders, But Not Their Fathers' Leaders

They want coaches who focus on augmenting people's strengths, inherent personality traits, and goals. Command and control has its place, but that place is pretty small and far in the distance.

## Constant Feedback Trumps Weighty Annual Reviews

In our always-on, social-feedback-laden culture, Millennials have grown up with constant streams of feedback informing them of their progress, likability, and marketability; waiting to find out "how I'm doing" in a quarterly or annual review simply does not work for this crowd.

This was one of the hardest things for me to master in my company after we started hiring Millennials in 2010. My previous experience with twentysomethings had been with young colleagues from the Gen X cohort, whom I felt were independent and didn't want a whole lot of participation from their managers (much to their detriment). My modus operandi was "If you haven't heard from me you are doing a good job." Adjusting to the palpable need for what seemed like constant feedback was a big hurdle.

In question-and-answer sessions following my workshops and presentations with intergenerational teams around the country, I continue to be asked why Millennials "need" so much feedback. *And my answer is: they just do.* So embrace the idea that your feedback—timely, constructive, and precise—is the gift you can give that keeps on giving and that ultimately it leads to people needing it less often. Truly, giving good feedback is a gift we give ourselves, because it yields exponentially more clarity among teams, better work product, and more cohesive teams.

As I described in depth in my first book, *Millennials & Management*, giving feedback "that people can actually hear, absorb, and act on is challenging for everyone." However, if you take the mind-set that no one *wants* to do a bad job and that people *want* their teammates to help them play the game to win—just as they would help their teammates score a goal—then giving precise feedback when it's most effective can become second nature. Note that the most effective timing is often not during a tight time crunch. It's much more effective to wait until deadlines have been met before reviewing what could have been better.

I encourage everyone to read Kim H. Krisco's *Leadership and the Art of Conversation*; in it, he shares how we can move from being talkers to being real communicators who lead from whatever seat in the boat we have.

Being proactive today, building skills for advancement, and being relevant for tomorrow weigh equally in any professional development plan—no matter your age or experience level.

A business without a Millennial is a business without a future, and if you can create an environment in which your Millennials thrive, your Gen Xers and Boomers will thrive too. Being a great place to be from means considering the framework that your youngest employees, who will soon make up more than half of the American workforce, have grown into.

## Now's the Time to Double Down

When you know an employee is going to leave—which you do the day you hire her—instead of retracting learning, training, and mentoring, you need to expand these vital components of your workplace culture.

From a purely practical sense, instead of worrying about good people leaving you, worry about mediocre employees staying, and do whatever you can to raise the "low" performer bar so that if higher-performing employees do leave you are not left with a mediocre, strategically disadvantaged workforce. Focus on ensuring that the "lowest" performer has the training, mentorship, and feedback loop he needs to improve and thrive. The byproduct of this approach will be that the higher-performing, "great" employees will stay longer in this type of environment.

> CFO: What happens if we train them and they leave?
> CEO: What happens if we don't and they stay?
>
> —business adage

# How to Green Your Own Pasture

Don't worry about people leaving. Worry about people staying. Move from fear of "wasting time" on training for disloyal employees to excitement around helping your employees find and use their strengths in your business. This creates the green grass on your side of the fence. If you don't water your own grass, any other grass will look greener.

It's almost as if employees are looking out at the world with green-colored glasses on, and all they see is better pastures everywhere else. Pay attention to greening your own grass, so that when people do look out they don't see greener they only see different.

## Mentoring

The number one request by Millennials in the workplace, worldwide, is help finding a mentor.[9] In my own research with U.S.-based Millennials, 73 percent stated that "getting a mentor" was "extremely important" to them. This isn't that surprising when you factor in that 55 percent of Millennials cite their parents as their best friends.[10] They are used to, and want, relationships with older people who will help them navigate their way.

A strong mentorship program need not be a "heavy," expensive, or overtly managed factor in your organization. Providing a natural structure or access path to mentorship is incredibly important for your younger employees, and it has tremendous benefits not just for the mentees but also for the mentors.

A good mentor–mentee relationship is one with clear boundaries and mutually understood responsibilities and time commitments. It might be one session over lunch. It might be a five-year relationship conducted only by e-mail. Whatever it is, the best mentoring is mutually beneficial and rewarding.

Older mentors should not expect their mentees to want to follow in their footsteps. As one fifty-nine-year-old senior executive in Minneapolis put it, "I had to get over the fact that my mentee didn't ask me to be his mentor because he wanted to become the next me—he wanted to make he sure he knew how to avoid what his perception of my life was. This was not the mentoring experience I wanted when I was his age. At the same time, I really enjoying working with my mentee, and I learned a lot from him too."

## Specific and Timely Feedback

As I said earlier in this chapter, I believe that every person, regardless of experience, title, or salary, wants to do a good job and that everyone's work can be improved. And very few of us want to live in a vacuum without feedback. Creating a culture where feedback is natural, constructive, and expected not only increases performance, but it also increases collaboration, team effectiveness, and morale. Set the expectation early (on day one!) that feedback is the normal course of business on your team. The key to constructive feedback—both positive and corrective—is specificity. "Great job" is nice to hear but not very helpful. Better is, "You did a great job summarizing the situation so that John could respond quickly," or "You really delivered that presentation well. You used your hands and body to help make your points and you didn't look at or just read off the slides. Great job."

Corrective feedback is also most effective when specific. Instead of saying "This is crap," say "This is not up to our standard or my expectation, and I want to show you how you can improve it to deliver what is needed. Let's talk later today for thirty minutes." Tone is critical if you want to be heard—you've probably just delivered a crushing blow to the person you need to correct. Putting a buffer between the time you deliver the news that the person's work needs dramatic improvement and the time you're going to help him gives the person time to absorb the news and then review his work to get a jump start on the working session.

Too often, we take the path of least resistance and either think "I'll just do it myself" or avoid the very specific feedback that helps people correct their work or build on their success. What feedback would help you do a better job? When have you thought you were on track, only to find out later that you were off base? How did that make you feel? Understanding who you're talking with and adjusting your style to the other person's so that he can hear you is the mark of a great leader.

## Professional Development

Along with "Why should I work here?" a regular question prospective employees ask in interviews today is "Where does this position lead?" They need to feel that working at your company or in your team will be beneficial and will lead to many opportunities.

Candidates are not just interested in what the possibilities are, though. They're equally interested in the professional development and training that will be actively available to them. And while each position has specific hard and soft skills required, one size definitively does fit all when it comes to professional development. Each employee now requires a personalized professional development plan tailored to where she is, where she wants to go, and, as importantly, where the business is going.

Managers and the people they are accountable for have equal responsibility to create development plans that keep employees productive, relevant, and on a path they want (if they are capable). Even if what they ultimately want is not possible at your organization, career development will pay off with more satisfied employees and higher-quality work. Don't worry about developing people "out of the company." Worry about supporting the employee in his quest for the life he wants (of course, this assumes that the employee does his part and has the initiative to execute the plan).

## Flexible Work

The push for work–life balance has been a constant theme for the American workforce over the last twenty years, going hand in hand with the push for gender pay equity. Women—mostly working mothers—have advanced the issue, demanding more flexible jobs and work hours out-side the bounds of the nine-to-five workday (which labor unions of the 1800s had won for blue-collar workers). All of these efforts have been moved forward dramatically by technology that allows virtual collabora-tion, constant contact, and instant worldwide communication.

But in practice, flexible work, which caters to the employee's pref-erences regarding the time and location of work, varies widely among organizations that profess a flexible schedule or location-independent philosophy. Work–life balance used to mean a clear break between two blocks of time, work time and life time, with the occasional ballet recital or band concert thrown in. In today's twenty-four/seven worldwide econ-omy, as knowledge workers, who tend not to work in "shifts," move back and forth from work to life responsibilities and among organizations, the divide has been rendered negligible or imaginary by technology.

Many Millennials I know and have interviewed are very comforta-ble moving in and out of "work" throughout their entire workday, going back and forth from work responsibilities to "life" responsibilities and enjoyments or pleasures. The attitude "Why do you care where or when I work?" is prevalent among Millennials chafing at traditional work boundaries. "Why shouldn't I be able to go to yoga at 4:30 p.m. if I log on later to get all my work done?" asked Jane, a twenty-seven-year-old sales associate in Los Angeles. "I've never missed a deadline, but still my manager harps on me for not being available during the 'regular' work day. What if I don't do my best work during the regular day?"

Other people prefer clear time zones for work and nonwork, and they struggle to create boundaries that allow them to work only during the traditional workday and not be on-call for e-mails and calls at all hours, seven days a week. There is no single, easy prescription that is suitable for all work environments. Just as a nine-to-five routine doesn't work for everyone, neither does the does the seemingly chaotic "work any-time, anywhere" philosophy suit every situation. However, the ability of a workplace to flex to accommodate the different responsibilities of its employees is critical to the company's ability to attract and retain top talent. If we all agree that top talent is an important indicator of success and sustainability, then we all must work to make it work at work for the employees who fulfill and achieve the business's goals.

## Caring for Children

It is ridiculous that the United States is the only Western country without paid leave for new parents. Ignoring the political implications of the issue, it should be obvious that finding ways to accommodate new parents with a combination of paid and unpaid leave is key to retaining both mothers and fathers. While working parents may not return to the workplace in the same capacity after they become parents, recruiting, onboarding, and training a new employee every time a woman gives birth is folly—both expensive and unnecessary.

We need to apply some imagination to figure out work responsibilities, compensation, and hours that don't just allow but facilitate our teams and find ways that every member can contribute fully, even if there is a ballet recital at 1 p.m. on the last Thursday before the end of the quarter. New working parents—who have really broken the mold—are relatively easy to plan for; the first five years of a child's life are predictable for the majority of kids—shots at six months, kindergarten at five years, and so on.

I counsel the working parents in my company to check their personal e-mail or the school's parent-activity websites two or three times a day to make sure they see school or parent-only communications. If you don't, you run the risk of getting stuck with the "worst" volunteer assignments at school events. When I was room mom at my older son's school (twice), I made sure I created the work sign-up sheets and I put my name in the "two dozen 2 x 2 brownies, no crust" cell before I sent the link on to other parents.

## Caring for Parents

The issue that businesses are starting to face in scale—and it's bigger than even the child-care issue—is that employees must care for their ailing, elderly parents or relatives. I started my company in 2002 when my sixty-four-year-old mother was diagnosed with stage-four lung cancer.

She and my father lived in Wisconsin, while I lived with my family in the San Francisco Bay area; one sister was in Boston and the other lived in Chicago. It was clear to me that if I wanted to be with my mother during her last days, I could not take one of the "regular" jobs I was in contention for at the time. I was going to require the flexibility to be where I needed to be, regardless of the situation at work—even as I was the primary breadwinner for my family. So I started Double Forte with my partner, Dan Stevens. Over the next three years I spent more than half of my time in Wisconsin. I learned firsthand how challenging it is to both earn a living and care for my ill mother. That hard-won learning has informed everything about our company's values and culture.

In 2014, within one month, seven of Double Forte's thirty-six employees found out that one (or even both) of their parents was critically ill. Within ten months, one of these parents had died. The impact to the team was much deeper than I could have ever imagined.

While accommodating employees who are pregnant or are caring for newborns or young children after they return to work can be challenging and requires different workflows, the pattern is relatively predictable. New parents returning to work had nowhere near the impact on our team that we faced when 20 percent of our workforce was in some way caring for a dying parent. That challenge is infinitely more complicated. And businesses need to work out now how they will get comfortable, flexible, and resourceful with a workforce that will increasingly be called on to care for critically or chronically ailing parents.

Deloitte, the multinational professional services firm, took a huge step forward last year when it acknowledged the tremendous responsibility its employees have in caring for aging parents. In September 2016, the worldwide consulting firm announced a dramatic broadening of its family leave benefit; it would grant any employee sixteen weeks of paid time off to support life events ranging from birth or adoption of a child to caring for a chronically or acutely sick spouse or elderly relative.[11] Of course, Deloitte is an international company with more than 240,000 employees. That company has many more resources at its disposable to field gaps left by employees who become caregivers. The impact on the small and medium-sized businesses that employ hundreds of millions of people in this country will be staggering as time goes on. We all need to learn to be flexible, because our turn is coming.

When our small company was handling the holes created by our seven colleagues' different caretaking preferences for their parents, communication and support were front and center for everyone. I am so thankful that our team did what came naturally, filling in to support teams so that the work did not suffer. At the same time, this is the picture of what is to come—at a huge scale—across the country.

## Deadline Management

If your organization is handling people who are planning to go to yoga at noon, a soccer game at 2 p.m., or chemo sessions with a parent for about eight hours on Fridays, the critical issue becomes establishing a deeply planted understanding among the workforce regarding deadlines and communication. Overt planning that takes into consideration each team member's preferred schedule must be driven by deadlines that don't burn anyone but that may require everyone to work at what used to be called irregular hours.

Flexible work requires inflexible deadlines that are specific—time, date, time zone—and consistently met. Practicing rigor around deadline planning will set your team free to accomplish all they want or need to while still achieving their business goals. No one said it was easy, but we know now that the "easy," standard, nine-to-five work hours do not work for the majority of the American workforce.

### Effective Deadlines

Effective deadlines are precise and specific: they state what time, on what date, in what time zone. Do not use terms open to interpretation, such as *end of day, later, next week*, or *tomorrow*. When are those times? I'll tell you when they are: never! To create the deadlines that keep our remote, virtual, always-moving-around teams on track, we need to shift from vague colloquialisms to very specific schedules, much as airlines and trains declare when their planes and trains are leaving.

Instead of "I'll give the next draft to you Friday," say "I'll give you the next draft in e-mail by 2 p.m. this Friday." If you're talking with someone in a different time zone, throw the time zone you're talking about in there, too: "I'll give you the next draft to you in e-mail by 2 p.m. Eastern this Friday." Being clear and consistent will dramatically drive up efficiency and drive down confusion and misunderstanding.

## Salary Progression

Another way to green your company's pasture is to examine and adjust salary practices. A practice of standard 3 percent raises every year, particularly for people in the first five years of their careers, basically ensures that your younger talent will look elsewhere, perhaps before they really want to, to make their salary increase appreciable. For knowledge workers, I recommend a graduated plan that has standard rates, commensurate with performance, in the 10 to 15 percent range until employees reach $75,000. After that, dropping the average raise to 3 to 5 percent yields appreciable gains; however, it's still important to ensure that your employees are paid at market rate so that good talent doesn't have to leave in order to be paid the median wage.

### Sample Salary Progression

| Starting salary | $ 47,500 | | Increase | $ 47,500 |
|---|---|---|---|---|
| 15% | $ 54,625 | Year 1 | 3% | $ 48,925 |
| 13% | $ 61,726 | Year 2 | 3% | $ 50,393 |
| 11% | $ 68,516 | Year 3 | 3% | $ 51,905 |
| 10% | $ 75,025 | Year 4 | 3% | $ 53,462 |

As one thirty-one-year-old marketing executive explained to me, "I left the company because I couldn't keep saying no to so much more compensation at the companies that were recruiting me. And when my company recruited me to come back two years later, I made a huge leap in salary even though my rank at the company was one step lower. If they had just adjusted my salary to the market rate I would have stayed and ultimately made less."

We know that companies' business models with regard to salaries will have to change dramatically if they are to be relevant in the future. I heard over and over again how companies are being penny wise and pound foolish with their compensation plans.

Of course, compensation is just one piece of the puzzle. As seen in figure 5.1 below, happiness at work is a product of greening your pasture - a holistic approach to high expectations and appreciation.

## The Happiness Factor

A green pasture is one that people enjoy staying in and returning to. Eventually, employees move to other pastures, but if yours is green, great

# Green Your Own Pasture

Market Rate Salaries

Professional Development & Coaching

Flexibility to Handle Work & Life Responsibilities

Specific & Timely Feedback

# Workplace Happiness

**Figure 5.1** Green Your Pasture to Create Workplace Happiness

people will stay longer and low performers will become higher performers faster.

Everyone is going to leave your organization someday. Don't worry about it. Your first responsibility is to ensure that while people are with you they have highly productive, constructive, and positive experiences, even in the face of tough situations and need for improvement. By taking care of your team and helping them improve, you are improving performance while you provide incredible value and experiences that employees will value throughout their careers.

Being a great place to be from means considering the framework your youngest employees have grown up with; when Millennials thrive, so do Gen Xers and Boomers, although the opposite is often not true. And it means being a happy place to work.

## Happiness at Work

Happiness and performance tend to go hand in hand. When you're happy, you spend less time worrying or perseverating about "what's not fair" and more time doing the work with energy, even joy . . . imagine!

Unhappy employees tend to be a drag on a team and bring down performance. That is why hedge fund guru Paul Tudor James, CEO of the Tudor Group, immediately liquidates his money from a fund if he learns that the fund's manager is in divorce proceedings.[12] Sugata Ray, of the University of Florida, has tracked hedge fund managers' performance and quantifies the drop in performance for fund managers going through divorce "to the tune of 7.4 percent. So if the average hedge fund's performance is maybe 10, 12 percent year, if they're good, you're losing two-thirds of that, annualized."[13] Of course, this is the extreme.

From a general work point of view, I have found that most inefficiency in the workplace comes from two sources: first, a genuine lack of understanding about the task at hand and, second, the time spent and the mistakes or poor performance that result from feelings of resentment, frustration, or underappreciation. The first is easier to address than the second. The second requires willingness to confront and resolve the issue driving the feelings that are generating the negative energy. A healthy organization is an optimistic one in which, maybe counterintuitively, conflict is regularly resolved without intervention from a third party or lots of time passing.

In fact, happiness at work is good business: Happy employees are on average 31 percent more productive, generate an average of 37 percent higher sales, and are three times higher in creativity.[14]

This isn't a new philosophy, it's just a less practiced principle because, in general, people don't like conflict or feel they will suffer negative consequences from it.

"New work"—the future of work—is more than just bringing your own device to work, working a flexible schedule, taking pauses during a career, or changing careers three or four times over a lifetime. The new expectation for work is happiness at work. This is particularly true, I think, for high performers.

**Hap • py:**
- Feeling pleasure and enjoyment because of your life situation
- Showing or causing feelings of pleasure and enjoyment
- Pleased or glad about a particular situation, event, etc.[15]

Most companies work very hard to hire and retain the best talent. Now, too, there is an increased push to hire high-performing, committed, and happy team players. Millennials are pushing this trend, leaders of all ages are pushing it, and our broader culture is pushing it. And while a company is not responsible for a person's whole happiness, businesses that thrive do take responsibility for ensuring that their employees are happy and committed to their positions.

For high performers who are either not committed or not happy, smart companies are making changes that result in happier, more committed team members; if an employee is still not satisfied, companies are working with that person to transition her out of the company in a mindful and respectful fashion.

Robert Glazer, founder and managing director of Acceleration Partners and an active EO (Entrepreneurs' Organization) member in the Boston chapter, together with his team, instituted "The Happiness Conversation," a new approach to employee development and relationships, in 2014. Based heavily on Ralph Dandrea's work "The Commitment Conversation,"[16] as well as on his own experience, Glazer's new approach has brought much success—and increased happiness—to his growing company. "I'm just unwilling to have a company where people don't want to be here or they are unhappy in their positions," Glazer said. "We believe we can create a culture where transitions are better, and are treated differently from what exists today at most companies."

This point of view sets the stage to create boomerang employees of all types—people who return as employees, contractors, partners, or customers. If you treat people well on the way out, you stand a chance of keeping them in your fold, to the benefit of your business over the long term.

No one wants to lose good employees, but if something is wrong in an employee's point of view that is fixable and you don't fix it, you've already lost her. You need to head off negativity or disenchantment so people don't get to the "unhappy" place without you knowing it, if it's possible. And if it's not possible to fix the things that are making certain employees dissatisfied given the framework of your business, then focus your energy on transitioning these people out of your workforce. They will still remain part of your company, they just won't be working for you anymore.

## The Happiness Conversation Is a Transformational Practice

I have been highly influenced by Glazer and Dandrea's efforts to create happier employees and what I share here is, in large part, based on their work. Productive, work-based happiness conversations require openness and honesty on the part of both employee and manager. If the conversation is to go well, the people involved and the company at large must understand their responsibilities.

## Create an Expectation of Happiness

A company's willingness to create an expectation of happiness, high performance, and conflict resolution, and its encouragement of the attitude that it is possible to fix issues, is critical to creating a happy workplace. The company's responsibility is to insist on the highest degree of confidentiality and to promise to work with employees who are doing their jobs but aren't satisfied or engaged before walking them out. Of course, the company has to provide recourse if the employee's unhappiness is generated from a challenging employee–supervisor dynamic.

## The Employee's Responsibility

The employee's responsibility is to share how she is feeling before her attitude starts to impact her performance. As Glazer explains, being unhappy "doesn't mean you want to leave or even have to leave; it just means something needs to change." These conversations can also turn into positive and productive career conversations that articulate a new path of opportunity and learning.

## The Supervisor's Responsibility

The supervisor must acknowledge and address work-related concerns that are brought to her in an authentic and open conversation. In this equation, supervisors who don't understand or actively seek out their team members' concerns aren't doing their jobs. It is the supervisor's responsibility to work with employees to lay out a path to resolving the issue or to foster career exploration, advancement, or transfer and to give employees a chance to fix any problem if they are underperforming.

## Two Questions

When seeking input from employees in these types of conversations, I encourage all supervisors to ask questions that probe their teammates' career goals as well as assess their interest in team participation. For instance:

1. What skills do you have that you wish you were using here?
2. What training would you like to build your skill set or advance your career?

The answers to these two simple questions will help supervisors keep their team members feeling fully utilized and identify the training their people want, in addition to whatever training they need to meet the changing requirements in their work and/or to stay relevant in their positions.

What happens when these open, honest conversations don't work and the high-performing employee decides she needs to go despite your best efforts?

## Willingness Isn't Happiness

"I don't want to do this work, but I'm willing to do this work" does not reflect an attitude that leads to success. Being willing but lacking enthusiasm and commitment is not the same as being excited and happy with the work or team at hand. It is the rare person who is unenthusiastic yet maintains the productivity and team camaraderie that high-performing teams require to work well.

At the same time, if you are not completely happy at work, it is important to realize that not everything will make you happy! In these cases, you need to understand what you can learn from the work and how it will benefit you over the long haul. There are many reasons to be interested in work, even if the subject matter doesn't get you out of bed in the morning. Find the silver lining in the work to get past "willing but not happy." Because if you're willing but truly not happy, it's time to go.

## The Mindful Transition

We already know that no employee stays forever, and, frankly, it is better for organizations to help their good and great employees transition out before they become less productive and become a drag on a team's performance and energy. You have an unhappy team member who is still a high performer, the most loyal thing he can do is initiate a mindful transition; the most loyal thing the company can do for this person is to initiate it if the employee doesn't.

Each mindful transition is different, crafted so that both the individual and the company benefit while the employee seeks his next step. Transition periods may be anywhere from 30 to 180 days, depending on the employee's and the team's workload. In return for the employee's positive action and for providing an intentional and respectful work transition for the team, companies can offer many things to demonstrate their dedication to their soon-to-be-gone employee. These things might include paid third-party career coaching, referrals to the senior leader's personal networks, and flexible work schedules that accommodate a job search as long as the work is being done. Do what you need to do to keep a committed employee until his last day and as long as he stays committed to follow-through.

"It may sound too good to be true," says Glazer, "but if we can change the traditional work–life paradigm, why shouldn't we take it a step further and change the employer–employee paradigm as well?"

# CHAPTER 6

# Being a Good Place to Be From

You don't want to keep every employee forever or contiguously for many years, of course. Sometimes, the talent you have isn't the talent you need any longer, as technology advances, markets change, or business models shift. Sometimes you make a hiring mistake; other times an individual stops pulling his weight or becomes a time and energy suck on the organization in comparison to his contributions.

People who don't contribute positively to the organization have to go. The longer you keep nonperformers, energy suckers, or toxic people in your organization, the more likely you are to lead good people to the door. Leaders who allow negative contributors to stay on the team engender less respect and loyalty from the positive contributors in the group.

No one said it's easy. What makes managing the transitions easier for the organization—and for both the employees you want to keep and those you need to prune—is clear and consistent communication about your company's philosophy regarding team composition, training, participation, moving on, and returning.

The reverse is true for employees, of course! People shouldn't work at organizations that don't advance their careers or help them meet their professional and personal goals. To forge the strongest relationship between great companies and great talent, we need to focus on creating companies that are great to be from and careers that move from one of these companies to another over time.

The way you treat those workers whose transgressions are not egregious but who simply aren't a good fit is critical to keeping everyone else on board.

### Pride in Your Company

Double Forte is, quite intentionally, a small company, and our "special sauce" is a combination of our culture, our high performance standards, our professional development program, and our proclivity for laughter. We keep Double Forte relevant by ensuring that our employees are desired by our competition. And we retain our employees by constantly greening our pasture so leaving for a competitor doesn't look as attractive as staying at the company. I meet with all new employees during their first week, and in that meeting I tell the person "I hope you stay a long time at Double Forte. But the most important thing to me is that you are proud to have worked here when you do move on."

## Being a Good Place to Be From

For the most sought-after companies, adopting an aggressive "move along" model yields a forward-leaning, high-performing staff. It also yields an impressive alumni base that is highly desired by other companies hungry for people who have contributed meaningfully to those high-flying companies. Of course, we are talking about organizations in leading and lucrative positions in growing categories, ones that have compelling missions and optimistic views of their futures. We can all learn from these types of companies.

Netflix, the world's largest Internet television network company, is one of the most sought-after places to work, according to LinkedIn's Top Attractors list, where it ranks eleventh among all U.S. companies.[1] Netflix is known not only as a sought-after employer but also for being a firing culture suited only to the best of the best performers. Unlike other tech or venture-funded companies that boast of perks like ping-pong tables, candy walls, nap rooms, soda machines, beer taps, and catered lunches, Netflix is candidly "low perk," preferring to load its compensation into high salaries based on top market performance.

Netflix's "culture deck"—which seems to have spawned copycat culture codes in companies of all sizes around the world—is what Facebook COO Sheryl Sandberg calls "the most important document ever to come out of the valley."[2] A PowerPoint document devoid of virtually all of the elements a professional presenter would require in terms of visuals, word count, and white space, the presentation called "Netflix Culture" has been viewed almost fifteen million times since it was published on SlideShare in 2009.[3] If you have not read this presentation, make sure you do . . . soon.

The slide deck was the brainchild of Patty McCord, Netflix's original chief talent officer, who famously eschewed traditional HR practices to create the tenets that would ensure Netflix's success. Under McCord, the company shifted from "tolerating" adequate performance to compensating such performance with "a generous severance package."[4] Moving to a model analogous to that of a pro sports team ensures Netflix has "stars in every position" who work well together to achieve. As the company's culture deck declares, "We're a team, not a family"[5] and "We help each other be great."[6]

That philosophy means terminating great employees who don't cut it with the rest of the high-performing team or who are made redundant by their own great work and/or new technologies, all in service of finding the best players for each position—positions that may change over time as the company's game changes.

During her tenure at Netflix, McCord, who was herself exited from the company based on her success and the company's evolution, "moved on" hundreds of employees and today calls herself the "queen of the good goodbye" even to hard-working people devoted to their company.[7]

One story about McCord exiting a great employee who had been replaced by automation encapsulates the Netflix philosophy. Netflix had articulated a product-testing automation strategy and set the wheels in motion to realize it. After some time, the strategy was fully implemented and the last person standing in the team was transitioned out of the company; that employee was disappointed by the decision after the hard work she'd put in. McCord called the employee to talk with her about the decision and reinforced her value and excellence while reiterating that the company no longer required her talents: "You're the best. You're incredibly good at what you do. We just don't need you to do it anymore." In that same conversation, McCord told her former colleague to "hold your head up and go be from Netflix."[8]

The sports team analogy Netflix uses is imperfect given that knowledge workers don't have the same grooming systems, player associations, or "farm" systems that professional athletes and leagues do, but it's interesting to consider nonetheless. In this framework, it becomes universally understood that the company requires the best talent for the job at hand at the right time in order to succeed. The need to let that talent go when that individual or team is no longer required or is no longer performing at the top of their game is equally important for everyone to understand. In knowledge-worker-based businesses, the only way this is possible over time is if the company is a badge of honor on a resume and implicitly carries tremendous weight in the recruiting process. And the standard of culture and compensation a company must maintian in order to attract and retain top talent to "pinch hit" for as long as they are useful is incredibly high.

The litmus test of success for Netflix? Netflix is a "good place to be from."[9] As several executive recruiters commented to me, "being from Netflix basically ensures your next, good, position." Here is the big lesson: Successful companies of the future will have legions of alumni who are proud to have those companies on their resumes—leaving or being "moved along" will be a positive, not a negative.

As Caroline Fairchild, new economy editor at LinkedIn, describes, "Unlike most tech employer campuses within commuting distance of the Bay Area, at Netflix you won't be hard-pressed to find someone over the age of 35 walking around the office. A company that famously claims to only attract 'fully formed adults,' Netflix demands self-sufficiency from employees and rewards them accordingly."[10]

Of course "fully formed adults" are usually not twenty-two, twenty-four, or twenty-eight years old; Netflix rarely hires recent college graduates, which means that other companies are providing the training that eventual Netflix employees need to be employed there. So, as much as Netflix creates great employees for other companies, it requires great employees trained at other companies in order to succeed. Netflix's position in Silicon Valley's ecosystem allows the company to continue this high-return business model.

The Netflix model hammers home the point that companies do not exist for their employees. Businesses exist to serve customers' needs, and over time customers' needs change. To continue to meet those needs, companies must constantly evolve. Whereas change may have taken place over a decade or two or three when our older colleagues were beginning their careers, it is now happening so fast we can see it today. And what was once a relevant skill set may have become obsolete. We are going to hear a lot more about losing white-collar jobs to automation in the next five years; what started as a trickle will become a fast-moving river by 2025, if not before.

## Training Relevance

Marshall Goldsmith's seminal business coaching book *What Got You Here Won't Get You There* remains an entrepreneur's and high-performer's bible on leadership growth and coaching. In it, he describes the myriad nuanced behaviors and habits that make the difference between getting to the position and being a well-respected, successful leader. I highly recommend reading, absorbing, and applying his principles, as Goldsmith does a masterful job at breaking down the qualities needed for the ascent versus those required in the leadership role. His very helpful process allows leaders to see where they fall short and how they need to shift to truly lead an organization of any size.

The principle encapsulated in Goldsmith's title can also be applied to your employees: The people who got your company to its current position are probably not the ones who will get you where you want to go. Or, at least, the skills those in your company needed to push your company to one position may not be the skills required to get it to the next, better position. And the rate of change for the required skills will only pick up speed in the coming years.

> The people who got you here aren't the ones who will get you there.

The increasing pace at which necessary work skills are changing has caught many Baby Boomers and older Gen Xers flat footed. Not only is length of service no longer valued, but the skills we need to remain relevant in our work must be updated constantly. Boomers who counted on their experience to keep them in a job will increasingly be disappointed by their ability to remain employed or be hired unless they keep their skills fresh and continually adapt to the changing needs of the workplace. Professions with continuing education unit (CEU) requirements designed to keep niche-skilled professionals up to date on advances in their fields have a significant advantage, career wise, over most white-collar and knowledge workers. There is no standard "relevance" training for management, no technical standards or industry knowledge requirement everyone needs to meet to stay qualified.

If you are running an organization, relevance is critical, and you must be willing to dedicate time to keeping yourself and your team relevant to ensure continuing profit. In a rapidly changing world, those legacy companies that are willing and able to innovate and invest in keeping their employees—in all positions—relevant are the ones that will not just survive but thrive. Business models are changing, and the more we hang on to the past, the more we ensure our demise. However, different dynamics in business are changing at different paces, and we will all need to straddle the old way and the new way for a while. But if your people are not willing to learn new skills, they will drag you down and cost you revenue, profit, and younger, more current talent.

Just because someone isn't right now doesn't mean he won't be right later.

# CHAPTER 7

# Leaving So You Can Come Back

Returning as an employee is dependent on two things: first, the company wanting you to return and, second, you wanting to return, with or without new conditions and understandings. And while it may be tempting to make a dramatic flourish like Tom Cruise as Jerry McGuire in the movie of the same name—including scooping a goldfish out of the company fish tank and inviting colleagues to a more satisfying future by saying "Who's coming with me?" followed by awkward silence broken only by Renee Zellweger's character saying "I will"—don't do it. Really. Do not do it.

Even if you leave a company feeling that you absolutely never want to return, you do not know what will happen in the future; those people you think you'll never cross paths with again may turn up as clients, customers, colleagues, or even hiring managers in a new company, either by hire or by merger.

The graceful exit is its own art form, and it is one that will pay off in spades over the life of your career. What you can control in this process is yourself, and once you've exhausted all recourse at your company, your effort needs to move toward making the best exit possible for yourself—and for your company, too.

## The Good Exit

The good exit is something we all have within our control. Even if your manager or supervisor is terrible and doesn't conduct himself professionally, do everything you can to set a high bar for behavior on your way out. The last impression you make is the one people will remember.

If you've made your career or life goals well known and done what you can to maximize them at your current company but the opportunities you want are not there, then having a "shot across the bow" conversation with a supervisor is appropriate, as long as your relationship is positive. Ask for a meeting to talk about your progress in your role. Prepare well for this meeting, and be ready to discuss your performance to date, where you've provided significant value, and what you would like to do in the next period of time. The conversation should have the following three distinct parts:

1. **A thank you and discussion of the recent past**
   - Thank the supervisor for taking the time to talk about your progress and aspirations.
   - Outline what you've achieved, what you've learned, and what you've helped other people learn since your last review.
   - Discuss where things haven't gone well and how you've adjusted to make a compromised situation better.

2. **An exchange about the future**
   - Discuss different ways you'd like to see your career evolve based on your experience. Do you want a promotion? Do you want to change responsibilities? Do you want to move from manager to individual contributor or vice versa? Be specific. If you see different possible routes, outline them.
   - Are there opportunities in your company that look interesting? Which ones, and why?
   - Ask for feedback from your manager: "I'd like your feedback on where you think I'm best suited" or "What do I need to do to make this next step possible here?"

3. **A talk about next steps**
   - It's a fifty-fifty chance that your supervisor will be able to help you realize your goals with the company you're already working for, even if you think you've exhausted your possibilities.

- If there really isn't a way to realize your goals within the team or the company, ask for recommendations. Keeping you in the extended fold of the company is a good thing for your supervisor; ask her "What do you think my next best step would be?"
- LISTEN.
- Depending on the conversation, choose a next step together.
- Thank your supervisor for the conversation. Indicate that you're going to think about the matter more fully, and reiterate that you are dedicated to your current job.
- If appropriate, say when you're going to talk again to put a period on the conversation. For example, say "I'm going to do some thinking about this in the next few weeks and I'll circle back by _____." Always give a specific date when referencing the future; refrain from using general terms such as *next week* or *later this month*, which are open to interpretation.
- End the conversation by referencing a current project you're enjoying: "Thanks again. In the meantime, I'm excited about Project Katana! We're making good progress, and I'm looking forward to showing everyone what's happening next week."

Now your supervisor is aware that you are looking at what's next, *and* you are focused on what's now.

### Tie Things Up in a Bow Before You Give Notice

You may be walked out the door the day you give notice, particularly if you are going to a competitor, but that doesn't mean you can't prepare fully for a positive transition.

- Before you give your notice, tie your projects up in a bow and outline how you recommend your work be redistributed while the team considers how to replace you.

- If you manage other people, write a one-page status update on each of the people who reports to you, including your recommendations for promotion, assignment changes, or development priorities.
- Articulate an end date. While some human resources professionals feel that the two-week notice is as endangered as the blue whale, it remains the professional, respectful standard. If you can provide a longer, valuable runway, offer that up.
- If you have a contract that stipulates that your employment will cover a certain period of time, whether the time that remains is six weeks or six months, be prepared for an earlier exit while also being prepared to stay for the full length of your contract.
- Replace yourself. Make a recommendation about how to cover your job responsibilities. Write a new job description that captures everything you do, both officially and "off the job description." If you'll be there for a bit, help interview for your replacement. Do everything you can to not leave a hole when you leave.

## Don't Be Stupid

PR agencies bill hundreds of thousands, if not millions, of dollars each year for counseling clients who hired people who behaved stupidly on their way out of their last job. Don't be the person who costs your new company time or money because you were stupid in exiting your previous job. Every time your name is searched on the Internet, your bad behavior will come up, and it can be hard, and often costly, to suppress. Even if your new company keeps you, finding the next job will be harder.

In my career, now spanning more than twenty-five years, I've been called upon to offer counsel on or handle more high-profile negative human resources-related situations than I can count, ranging from theft of company intellectual property to extensive porn viewing to product sabotage, all discovered at the previous employer after the employee left. In most of these situations, I and my team have been called upon to handle the repercussions for both the company and the former employee, as these problems have significant potential to be distracting at the low end and highly detrimental at the extreme.

Based on my experience cleaning up what I generously call foolish mistakes by employees, I give you a list of things you should and should not do as you plan to exit a company:

- Do maintain your regular hours at work.
- Don't wipe your computer of any company documents.
- Don't download anything confidential from your computer—that's stealing.
- Don't sabotage a deal, a product, a person, or a partnership.
- Don't abandon your job during the notice period.
- Do adhere to company policies during your notice period.

Hopefully, you've kept personal documents and communication off your work computer. Remember, in most cases, anything on your company computer—including your Internet search history and your personal e-mail or photos—belongs to the company by virtue of the fact that it resides on company property. If you do have personal files on your computer, remove them, but don't be surprised if the company keeps them in its backup systems.

If you are using personal Dropbox, Box, or Google Docs accounts for your work, ask your IT department how you should dispose of these folders and files, and then follow those instructions.

Don't be stupid. Enough said.

It's tempting to just "phone it in" once you've given your notice, but resist that urge. Show up, do your job well, and facilitate your transition.

## When It's Their Call

If you've been exited from the company, well or poorly, it's important to demonstrate your professionalism by leaving as skillfully as if you had made the call yourself. I know it's hard—I've been there, twice. Do it anyway. Don't leave a bad taste in your soon-to-be-ex-colleagues' mouths by dropping out or making them work harder during your last days on the job. You don't know where those people will end up. Keep it professional: Show up, do your job, and provide recommendations even if you think they'll be ignored.

## The Perfect Exit

Modeling the perfect ending: I started Double Forte with a partner, Dan Stevens; we had worked together previously and enjoyed a great working and personal relationship. The first time he left Double Forte, he exercised his contract to maximize his buyout, with six months' notice. When he came to talk with me about this, he laid out a plan to replace himself, and then we proceeded to work that plan.

Dan returned to the company a few years later and stayed for four more years. He then came to me again with his goal to work at a high level in an international firm, which he knew I did not aspire to. This time, he planned a six-week time frame. By the time he had moved on to the large office of an international agency down the street, we had promoted two people, reassigned another two, and hired a senior person to fill the leadership void he would leave.

## Doors Close Forever

Human resources files around the country are strewn with stories of terrible employee exits that damage those employees' reputations for a lifetime. Even in today's litigious environment, which effectively limits references to "Yes, he worked here" together with dates and titles, the back-channel stories of unprofessional departures move quickly and widely, and they can limit a person's job opportunities for years to come.

> I had a boss who ended up being exited out of the company. He was given the opportunity to say it was his idea with more than two months' transition time. I never would have known that he was actually fired until he stopped showing up. His boss called me looking for something my boss had told his boss he had done, because the deadline had passed. Not knowing the situation I told my boss's boss that the work wasn't done yet, and I had been assigned that specific project the day before. It was not a good situation. Then, when my boss's boss had to reconstruct the work, all this other stuff came out. I hope I never get called about him; I don't know what I would say. I know I'll never work with him again . . . something that I don't think I would have said when he first told us that he was leaving.
>
> —Lisa, a middle manager at a
> San Francisco agency

As David Lewis, president of Operations Inc., a Connecticut-based human resources consulting firm, shares, recruiters are "going to think twice" if they hear an employee "handled his exit extremely poorly," even if that person had had a neutral to positive tenure at the company.[1]

Even worse is the reference call that does not get returned. After more than twenty years as a manager or leader of other people, I don't need two hands to count the people I would not return a reference call for— but given the number of calls I do return every year, my "silence is deafening," as one CEO told me when I didn't return his call about a former employee. That person was not hired.

### Memory Is Long

My older son attended Interlochen Arts Academy for high school so he could seriously pursue his music. Part of parent orientation is a meeting with the department heads of each division; for me, that was a meeting with Dr. Kedrick Merwin, director of the music department, and about one hundred other music majors' parents. First, he told us that our kids were all the "best harmonica" players at home, but that there is only one first chair at Interlochen for each instrument. *(I think this is much harder on many parents than it is on the kids, who seek to be among the best and know that they will be challenged by their new schoolmates, unlike at home.)* The second key point he made was that Interlochen fosters respect and support among the musicians. Merwin said, "You never know who will be auditioning you in the future, and you don't want them to pull the blind away after you play and have your heart sink because you were 'mean to that kid' at Interlochen. Here, your child will learn how to be a supportive and competitive colleague." Memory is long.

When you are on your way out of a company, don't:

- Talk badly about your boss or the company
- Play practical jokes (put salt in the sugar shaker, subscribe your boss to lots of magazines, take the hinges off the refrigerator door)
- Wear an offensive T-shirt on your last day
- Play an explicit or negative soundtrack that other people can hear . . . really.

## The Exit Interview

Most companies today will ask for an exit interview unless they walk you out the door the day you give notice. Advice on how to handle the exit interview varies widely among career advice coaches and experts.

The exit interview is a formality at large companies, something that HR has to do. Play nice. This is not the time to air grievances, no matter how constructive. Why? You have no control over what goes into the file or who will see it after you're gone. Years later, some other person may have to refer to your file to verify your employment, and you have no control over who that person is or how professional he will be.

At smaller companies, depending on your relationship and who conducts the interview (if there is one at all), you may feel more leeway. Use that leeway with caution, as you don't have control over how the information will be shared, maintained, or accessed once you have left the building. Some guidelines for positive exit interviews include the following:

- Refrain from reiterating concerns you have brought up in the past; definitely don't air new grievances.
- End on an affirmative note by saying something positive about what you've learned during your time at the company.
- Explain the reason you're leaving, briefly, in terms of your career goals and how your new position helps you fulfill them.
- Don't say too much about your new job.
- Consider what you will say if the company counteroffers with an enhanced salary or position. My recommendation: Politely decline and offer to help recruit your replacement from outside the company. Rejecting your new employer before you get there can have lasting negative implications for you.
- Say that working for the company has been a good experience and that you're proud of your work there.

## The Goodbye for Now

A short, well-written "goodbye for now" e-mail or note lets you leave with the sentiment you want. Don't forget to let people know how to reach you. Consider setting up a new personal e-mail account specifically for professional contacts.

Once you've left a company, it's up to you to maintain the connections there, even if the company has a good corporate alumni program. Not every former colleague is someone you'll want to actively stay involved with. Human nature and all that.

To manage your connections going forward, create three lists:

1. The people you'd work with again without question
2. The people you'd be interested in working with again under the right circumstances
3. The people you'd never work with again

Group 1 is probably going to be the shortest list; group 2 will likely be your longest list. As you are making your exit, take the following steps to ensure that you maintain your valuable contacts:

- Make sure your LinkedIn profile is up to date and that you've connected with all the people in group 1 and group 2. Accept invitations from people in group 3, but don't reach out to them.
- When you land at your next position, e-mail those people in groups 1 and 2 with the news.
- Consider how you will keep connected to everyone on the list of people you'd unequivocally work with again and those you'd work with again in the right circumstances.
  - Coffee/meal one or two times per year
  - E-mail with relevant articles
  - Trade shows and conferences
  - Walk and talk with those on your shortest list of people one to two times per year
  - Host a meetup or dinner once or twice a year with your choice of former colleagues

As a guideline, if you're thirty or older, plan to do something once a month with people on your group 1 list. If you're forty or older, maintain your network by scheduling something once a week.

## Be a Good Network "Partner"

Staying relevant and valuable to your former employer and colleagues is not just about your performance in your next job or the job after that. Keeping your options open for future employment, partnership, or contracting with your former company is predicated on being a valuable and connected former employee. Valuable former employees are people who find ways to advance the company's mission. For example, someone might be valuable because he:

- Refers business to his former employer, as appropriate
- Recommends qualified people for jobs at his former employer
- Creates informal partnerships with former employers. For instance, he
  - Asks a former colleague to be on a panel at a conference
  - Invites a former colleague to be a guest blogger on his new company's blog
  - Introduces a reporter to his former employer for relevant stories

## When You Didn't Leave Well

Regret often sets in after you've left poorly. Sometimes people realize that if they had conducted themselves better, then their old employer or colleagues could be business partners. Other times, they realize they were wrong and that their idealistic vision of the work world is even further from reality in their new position than it was in their former position. Or the bad manager or toxic colleague leaves the company, and they can imagine working there again. But a poor exit bars employees from acting on these revelations.

I encourage you to do repair work if you feel you left poorly, but only if you can do so authentically. Extending the olive branch or apologizing goes a long way in reducing or eliminating any negative perceptions or feelings your former colleagues may have. At the very least, you will feel better for having made the effort.

If, during a moment of anger or disillusionment, you wrote a negative review on any of the job review sites such as Career Bliss or Glassdoor, fix it or delete it. Even if the comment was anonymous, change the review; no one is really anonymous, and any change to the positive will be noted. (Remember that everything online is trackable by someone, particularly if you used a company computer or network to compose or upload your review.)

Once you have decided you want to repair damage you may have done, identify the people who matter most to you, and then make that list longer. Next, chart a plan to reestablish relationships with those people.

### Invite the Person to Coffee

Consider inviting your old boss or a former colleague to a thirty-minute coffee meeting to catch up. Assuming that person says yes, start the conversation with an apology and a thank you: "Thank you for having coffee with me. I was nervous to reach out to you, but I know that I didn't handle myself very well when I left the company, and I wanted to apologize to you. I'm sorry for any problems I may have caused."

Depending on the person's reaction, the issue may be closed or you may have more repair work to do. Listen carefully to what your guest has to say. Take it in. If that person is mad, let him be mad. If that person is hurt, let him be hurt. If that person forgives you, accept his forgiveness. This is the beginning of a new phase of your relationship. You are responsible for making sure it gets off on a good foot, and it's not about you. It's about how the other person feels about you. That person may need some time to process what you've told him. You've been thinking about this for a while; he may have dismissed the entire situation, or not—let him catch up to you.

Regardless of how the conversation goes, end with "Thank you for meeting me. Please let me know if I can do anything to help you. I hope we can go forward on a positive note."

After the coffee meeting, write the person an e-mail or note thanking him for getting together and restating your hope that you can go forward in a constructive way: "Thanks, Bill, for having coffee with me. I really appreciate our conversation and your willingness to listen. I hope we can go forward on a positive note. Please let me know if I can do anything for you. Best regards, Jill."

If the person does not accept your invitation, write a personal note and send it to the office. In it, apologize and state your intention to repair your relationship (see Figure 7.1).

I know this sounds hokey. If you don't mean it, don't do it. If you do want to make the effort, make the effort. People remember effort and appreciate those who actually do something to fix an uncomfortable situation. To counter one bad action, you may need a hundred good actions, but start somewhere.

## Network for the Person

Prove to your former colleague that you are genuinely sorry by doing things that he may find helpful without expecting anything in return, such as the following:

- Send an article that would be interesting or helpful.
- Introduce him to a candidate who may be a great fit for his team.

> Dear Tom,
> I understand your not wanting to grab coffee and talk with me—I get it. I wanted to apologize to you personally for leaving so poorly —I'm very sorry for any trouble I may have caused. Please know that I understand what I did was unprofessional and hurtful, and I am resolved to never let that happen again. Please let me know if I can help you in any way. I'd always welcome the chance to get together.
>
> Best regards,
>    Mike

**Figure 7.1** Sample Bridge-Building Note To Former Colleague

- Refer business to the person when appropriate and without any expectation of compensation.
- Invite the colleague to a group function you are hosting.
- Send him a business book you think he might enjoy.

## You're the Boss, and You Didn't Handle an Employee's Departure Well

Every boss I've talked with has a story or two or three about not reacting well when someone on her team left the company. Good leaders learn from their mistakes and improve. As the leader, your words and actions have incredible impact, not only on the former colleague but on your current ones. Repairing a broken relationship is a powerful lesson for everyone on your team, and admitting fault goes a long way toward earning trust and loyalty from the people around you. And the most important fault to rectify is the one that harms other people.

### Fixing It from the Top

John is a forty-five-year-old CEO of a four-year-old venture-backed company. He has a direct style that leaves no one free from conflict intended to drive to resolution—there isn't a lot of couching language or behind-closed-doors discussion. John's company is in the process of pivoting from a highly competitive market subject to commoditizing pricing pressure to a business model that will allow the company to better leverage its intellectual property and technical advantage. In the middle of this 180-degree turn, several key personnel jumped ship because of the grueling hours and the dramatically deferred payoff for their work; sensing blood in the water, head hunters had aggressively recruited these employees.

John did not respond well or quietly to the fact that some of his key talent was leaving the company, which had negative repercussions on the staff who were staying to help make the plan a reality. Understanding this, John reached out to the former employees to repair his relationships with them. As one of his colleagues told me, "He said it was humbling and hard, but that he couldn't move on with the team in good faith if he hadn't done what he could to make his relationships with those guys whole."

## Invite the Person to Lunch

If you're the boss, I recommend inviting your former colleague to lunch, not coffee as I recommend for the employee; the extra time away from the office is its own demonstration of your contrition. Thank the person for coming and apologize for not handling yourself well during her departure: "Thank you for coming, Sheila. I wanted to apologize for not handling myself very well when you gave me your notice. I'm sorry that I was not supportive and for causing you any trouble during your exit. I hope that I can repair our relationship."

Articulate what you wish you had done better and what you've learned from the situation. If, in response to the person's departure, you've made any changes to improve yourself or the organization, let her know and thank her for the inspiration. Ask the person about her new position and what she likes about it. Don't ask her to share anything negative with you.

At the end of the meal, thank the person again for having lunch with you and end with a positive statement, such as:

- "I've really learned a lot from this situation and am working to improve the way I handle disappointment. You've made a big difference for me."
- "Please know that you are welcome back to the company in the future."
- "Please let me know if I can help you in your current job."

After lunch, send a follow-up note or e-mail reiterating your conversation and the positive statement you left with.

## Recognize the Employee's Contribution

In some companies I've worked with or for, it's been taboo to talk about former employees' contributions after they've left the building. Don't let this be your culture.

The people "left behind" know how their former colleague did or did not contribute to the culture, a project, or the leadership team; if current employees know their work won't be honored after they've left, you are undermining your attempts to engender loyalty while they're still employed!

Also, even a simple statement such as "Before Cory left he made sure that the team was set up to succeed, I really appreciate the effort he made" goes a long way. You are demonstrating that your recognition transcends tenure, which is the whole point! And the statement you make will get to Cory quickly, carried by one of his former colleagues. Cory's realization that he's still appreciated even though he's not there anymore is step one in keeping him tied to the group and the company.

ServiceRocket, the cloud-based software training company, has regular all-hands meetings in each of its offices around the globe. CEO Rob Castaneda leads these meetings in whatever local office he's in, together with the office lead. Wherever praise is due it's given, whether that person is still at the company or not. "I want all the good employees to come back somehow, sometime," Castaneda said. "So I make sure they know we still appreciate what they did while they were here—the fastest way to do that is to share good stuff about those people with the people who are still at the company when it's relevant."

## Recruit the Person or Help Her Network

When a position opens that you think would be good for the former employee, in that it presents a better opportunity for her based on what you know, do not be shy about reaching out to her. Ask to get together to catch up, and share with her what's going on at the company.

Once you're together, describe what's changed or planned for the future for the company and the new position. Tell her that you think she would be perfect and want to know if she'd be interested in returning for this position.

## How I Came Back

One of my first jobs was at The Weber Group in Cambridge, Massachusetts. In the early 90s the company expanded to northern California and I wanted to move. I approached my bosses with my wish to transfer to the Palo Alto office and was told that, yes, I could move there, but I'd have to wait six months and help them replace me on my team in Cambridge. I deflected all recruiting calls as I did what they asked. At the four-month mark I approached them again with an eight-week countdown calendar and was told that I couldn't move, that my clients wouldn't like it.

I was pissed.

I went back to my desk and called all of the recruiters I'd shut down and told each of them that I wanted to get to California. I moved to Los Angeles nine weeks later. And five people called me within my first two months at my new position to help them move, too. I had no compunction helping four of them follow me to that agency.

Seven years later my former supervisor, now the president, asked me to lunch to explore whether I would come back to expand The Weber Group's business dramatically in San Francisco. We had a frank conversation that got my departure—and the departures of the four people who followed me—out of the way, and in the next month we came to an agreement.

If she says yes, talk more formally about the position and how it will be different from the one she left. Ask what she'd need to ensure her success. Make sure you address what both you and she would want to be different if she returns. Be realistic. You may not be able to accommodate her wishes; on the other hand, you might. Recruit her; don't assume she's doesn't need some wooing.

If she says no, ask if she has a recommendation from inside or outside the company. Listen and follow up on her suggestions. Even if none of these people gets the job, your attention to her recommendations will strengthen her ties to you and the company.

If you are leaving a company, it's up to you, the employee, to make it as positive an experience as possible, even if it wasn't your decision to go. Do everything you can to ensure your colleagues are well prepared for your absence, and don't leave any messes for them to clean up after your departure. Nothing negates positive feelings for a former colleague faster than being left holding a bag of unfinished work or unfulfilled promises. If your boss is negative about your departure, take the high road, even if it requires a virtual oxygen tank to stay at a high altitude.

What's important to keep in mind is that people will remember how you left, regardless of a positive or negative climate in the organization, and it's that memory that will help determine the way further opportunities come to you from former colleagues who either stay with that company or go elsewhere.

# CHAPTER 8

# Boomeranging in Practice

Boomeranging fully—coming back to a company as a full-time employee—has many advantages for the company as well as for the employee. For the employee, the advantages range from knowing what to expect to being able to focus on the job at hand without wondering "how good it is" elsewhere to being happy to being back on "their" team. The benefits for the company include a faster ramp to productivity, quicker cultural assimilation, and, perhaps most importantly, the message the rehire sends to the current workforce: "It's not so great out there after all; we've got it pretty good."

Other benefits to bringing employees back to the company include the new points of view and fresh ideas they garnered during their experiences outside the company walls. And, as Erik Charles, Xactly's vice president of product marketing, wrote on the company's blog: "There is an energy that comes from someone who is happy to return, and an employer can embrace and leverage that energy."[1] Charles himself had boomeranged back to Xactly, a California-based incentive solutions provider, after a little more than a year away.

Boomeranging is beginning to replace contiguous long-term tenure for much of the workforce. Indeed, even considering returning to a former employer is increasingly popular: Monster's 2016 poll revealed that while 30 percent of its respondents had actually boomeranged to a former employer, 51 percent of respondents would consider it.[2] This is evidenced by the hiring rate of former employees in the workplace: 40 percent of HR professionals surveyed by the Workforce Institute in 2015 hired "about half" of the former employees who applied to open positions.[3] This is a staggering statistic, and it represents a sea change in sentiment and workforce practice since 1998, when I was ridiculed by associates and colleagues for returning to work for The Weber Group after eight years away.

Culture has everything to do with why great employees want to return to their former employers. PwC, the global audit and consulting company headquartered in London, is a model for boomeranging employees. In the United States, 17 percent of its more than forty-six thousand employees working in more than eighty offices are Boomerangs. As Carl Rosenblatt, a boomerang executive in the Washington, D.C., office said in an interview, the PwC culture of work that is "systematic and dependable" and the "camaraderie" among his colleagues "makes coming to work fulfilling and enjoyable."[4]

The benefit to the employee at the highest level is being in a place where she feels honored and valued. Janet, thirty-five, a product manager in Boston, says "I didn't understand how positive my workplace was until I left it. When I came back, it was such a relief to be in a supportive environment."

## It Wasn't a Rut

After twelve years at one of the largest consumer and business e-commerce companies, Amy was lured away by a mobile and social game company. Amy said:

> I felt like I was in a rut and I was tired of how long things took to get done . . . the processes were the death of me. I shared my frustrations with my supervisor, who did his best to help me, but in the end I'd been there for twelve years. The new company

dangled lots of shiny carrots to get me to join the company—
bigger role, better salary, being a more important contributor in
a start-up, an IPO, fast-paced—they hit every hot button I had.
It looked hip, more fun, fast paced, so I took the position.

I knew the first day it was terrible. The culture there was
awful. The people weren't nice—it was incredibly toxic; no
one helped each other. People were expected to work around
the clock, even though they'd promised a flexible work schedule. People were quitting all the time without jobs—that's
the real tell, when employees leave without a new job locked
down.

Amy described her six months at this mobile game company as
"hellish" and "destructive," but as the primary breadwinner in her
family of four, Amy felt she was not in a position to quit her job
without securing a new one. She reached out to her former boss for
advice, and he promptly offered to help her return to the company.
The next day Amy was yelled at one last time. "I realized then that no
job was worth it," she said. "I was miserable; therefore, my family
was miserable. I quit in frustration that day without a job to go to."

Within three weeks, Amy had returned to her former company
with the help of her former supervisor. She took a position in a different department, which felt "kind of new. It was like visiting family
in Europe. It felt comfortable but not too close. The processes were
familiar, the flooring was familiar, the café was familiar, but no one
knew everything about me." And while her new position was a pay
grade lower, her new position has a higher salary than her previous,
higher ranking, position. And she picked up her benefits at the same
rate since she'd been gone less than two years. "I felt like I had to
eat a little crow since I didn't make it work at the gaming company,
but I am really happy for the lessons I learned while I was away. And
now the processes don't drive me as crazy as they used to."

Most returning employees see an appreciable bump in salary compared with what their salary would have been had they stayed, given the 3 to 5 percent raises standard in the annual review cycle (more on how to fix this in chapter 4). "The only way to make real money is to leave and come back," says Julie Lopez, a senior relationship manager for one of the largest search engine companies, who is based in New York City. "When I returned I got a 40 percent increase—they could have saved themselves a lot of hassle just by keeping my salary competitive."

Some companies go much further for returning employees, including bridging the benefits impacted by tenure. "When I returned to the company, my accruals for vacation and sabbatical picked up right where I left them, so I started out earning more vacation than newbie employees who started the same week I did, and was only a year and half away from being able to take my sabbatical," said Suzanne, a product manager at a large online payment company.

While none of the companies I interviewed would share their HR policies on the record, anecdotes told by returning employees indicate that vacation and sabbatical accruals often pick up right where the employee left them, with little price paid for the time away.

## Fast Ramp in Fast-Changing Markets

While fast onboarding is a benefit for virtually every employee who returns to a former company, during leadership transitions companies and their boards should seriously consider the advantage of bringing back a senior leader when markets are changing fast and company and industry relationships are critical for fast maneuvering. Such was the case for KQED Public Media, which operates Northern California's primary public media radio and television stations and has the largest public media audience in the United States.

When the CEO announced his retirement in 2009, the KQED board of directors launched a national search to replace him. An exhaustive search led KQED to offer the position to John Boland, who had left KQED four years previously to become the first chief content officer at the Public Broadcasting Service (PBS).

"When I left KQED, I never thought that I would return to work here in any capacity," said Boland. "Now, I can't imagine having been able to do all we've done in the last few years without leaving and returning." By moving to the national stage for one of KQED's key content providers, PBS, Boland was able to gain experience and visibility that he has deployed for KQED's advantage as CEO. At the same time, he reentered KQED with strong relationships with the majority of the senior management and much of the board of directors. "We made big changes pretty quickly that would have taken much longer to implement if I had not known the players so well," added Boland.

## How to Come Back

While the old adage "You can't go home again," made famous by Thomas Wolfe's posthumously published novel of the same name, may hold true for returning to the place where you grew up, it's not true when we're talking about returning to a company where you once worked. (Published in 1940, Wolfe's book explores American culture of the 1920s and 30s, delving into the impact of the stock market crash, the prevailing illusion of prosperity, and the changing dynamics between people and jobs and society—a novel worth a reread given the realities of our time.)

If you are an employee considering a return to your former place of work, you may be excited to go back to a company where you understand how things are done, but "it's important to understand that organizations are living organisms"; they won't be the same as when you left, no matter how short your time away, explains Heather Hawkins, a former vice president at Double Forte who boomeranged first as a client and then as an employee over eight years.

In evaluating your return to a former employer, "Do the same due diligence you would in reassessing the role and organization before reentering that you would do when accepting a wholly new role," says Hawkins. "This discipline will help ensure a good fit for who you've become and what the company has evolved to."

Important questions to ask when considering returning to a former employer include:

- What is different in this department/company/structure since I left?
- I know that John and Jane have left [note who else has left the company]; how did you shift things around with those departures?
- Have any significant changes in leadership or direction taken place? What's been the net effect?
- When I left, the direction was XYZ; how has that evolved? What's the view of the future?

It's important to help your former employer understand your current skills before you sign the offer letter. Unless you are expressly returning to the same position you held previously, with the same requirements and expectations, make sure that your employer understands what is new on your resume and in your skill set so that you don't get pigeonholed into what you were instead of what you've become in your time away.

Plan to ask a series of questions that illustrate your new skills and your enthusiasm for contributing in a different, more valuable way this time around. For example:

- When I left here, I was able to put my skills to work immediately at [the next company], and I've built those skills up quite a bit. How do you see me contributing if I return?
- I've really expanded my skill set since I left here, and I want to ensure that the company recognizes my growth and doesn't just

slot me into the position I had before. What's the process to make sure people understand my new role?

- Now that I've been gone from the company for a few years, I have a lot of ideas I think might be very beneficial to the company. How can we make sure I'm able to contribute in this way?

You should also assume that your particular brand of personal "baggage"—what may be noted in your personnel file or held as common understanding by your former colleagues—will come along with you as you consider rejoining a former employer. Were you a "hoverer" or "loud" or "too quiet" or "emotional" or "brusque" or something else? Be ready to address that head on in your exploration, and be prepared to counter any issues that come up in an open, never defensive, manner. Ask questions such as the following:

- From your point of view, why am I a good candidate for the job?
- Do you have any concerns about hiring me back to the company?
- What can I tell you about how I've changed since I left?

And of course, while companies are more willing to hire former employees today than they have been at any time in the past thirty years, it is not unusual to encounter bias against a rehire. Address these questions directly, as follows:

- What concerns do you have about hiring former employees in general?
- What concerns do you have about hiring me, specifically?

With more former employees applying to companies where they've worked before, a new set of criteria informs the recruiting process. While hiring managers may jump former employees to the front of the line in the recruiting process, it's important to also assess why returning is attractive and what new perspectives, skills, and potential Boomerangs bring to the table. As a manager considering rehiring a former employee, probe the following topics:

- Tell me how your experience at [new company] met the expectations you had when you left here.
- What were the big surprises you had at that position?
- What did you appreciate most about our company once you'd been gone for a while?
- What changes have you seen from the outside? What's your take on them?
- When you were here last, the company was struggling with XYZ; how do you think we've handled that?

Also, be explicit about whatever changes you expect from the employee and address any concern you have about a short tenure:

- In your last six months here, I noticed _____. I want to make sure we get off to a positive start and come to an agreement about how we will make sure we have a more productive relationship. Do you have any suggestions?
- What would you want to be different in this tour of duty?
- What would make you look for a new job?

## The Reentry

While returning employees may have an easier entry into organizations they've worked for previously, companies and their returning heroes should not assume the return will be seamless. The reentry is as important as the exit for Boomerangs returning to companies as employees. One, you have changed; two, the company has changed.

In addition to product marketing VP Erik Charles, Xactly has had more than twenty boomerang employees among its high-ranking executives in the past decade. Bernie Kassar, Xactly's chief customer officer, was first at the company for seven years, and he assumed increasing responsibilities during that period. His advice when reentering a former employer? "Be humble. Treat your new position as an entirely new job, because things do change when you leave." During your absence, Kassar notes, "other people have grown, assumed new roles, taken on new responsibilities—maybe your responsibilities. You need to honor what's happened while you were gone."

Just as you want people to see you differently based on the experience you have gained, you need to the see the company as it has evolved without you. "Companies grow—not just in size," says Michelle Curran, a Double Forte vice president who returned to the company after eight months at a different firm. "Realize it's not the same place you left that you are going back to. Share your learnings and encourage the good." While the onboarding process will probably be dramatically faster than for a never-before employee, don't take it lightly.

If you've had an expedited hiring schedule, it's critical that you take the time to make sure that your new team understands what you've learned while you've been elsewhere and how you can bring that to bear for the company and team. What was good about the place you've just left? What did they do well? What do you think would be useful for your current position? "I lived an entirely different career while I was gone," says Maura Wilchens. "I was able to bring new insight, experience, and a different point of view back to the company with me. I appreciated that the company didn't treat me as the same person I was when I left, and wanted to know and apply what I had learned."

Equally important is to talk about what you really appreciate about your company with the benefit of outside eyes and the experience you've had in the interim. This helps people understand why you are returning and gives them the benefit of your experience, perhaps solidifying their desire to stay at the company. Wilchens says, "I was able to share my experience—which was terrible—with my team and bring the benefit of that other job to my colleagues. It's easy to take for granted the things that are natural in one environment. When I saw that what makes my company special is really different, I had a totally different appreciation for what the company does to make it a great place to work, and I was able to reinforce that with my colleagues."

Insist on a formal onboarding process. Don't assume you know what the company has done in your absence. And don't assume everyone will be thrilled to have you back.

"It's really critical to respect what's happened while you were gone," says Kassar. "Other people assumed your responsibilities when you were gone, so honoring that is important when you return—try not to step on toes." Kassar acknowledges that he was "lucky, that I've had nothing but good will" since he returned to Xactly. At the same time, he says, "I'd be kidding myself if some people weren't apprehensive. Because I had a new, bigger role, we were able to work together to make sure the team is working better together than when I wasn't there. But I had to earn it."

## Be Proactive

What did you intensely dislike when you were at the company before? What constructive criticism do you have for the company you're returning to? This time around, what do you need to do to demonstrate that you are an evolved employee? Before you start your new position at your old company, review your reviews and come up with a new plan for how you're going to show up fresh and not fall into any preconceived pattern that potential detractors may be apprehensive about.

One of the reasons the CEO and president wanted me to return to The Weber Group was because I am a self-starter; I get stuff done on my own. Because the position was three thousand miles from HQ, the company needed someone who didn't need a lot of hand holding. At the same time, opening an expansion office that I would lead was an investment for The Weber Group, and not everyone was happy that the company had hired me for the expansion rather than moving someone from the

East Coast, or even Palo Alto, to the San Francisco office. I talked these things through with my boss, Marijean Lauzier, before I started, and she gave me a lot of rope to swing from. She didn't prescribe anything except "make it happen." I created a weekly progress form that I shared so that leadership (many of whom were still at the company from my first tour of duty), finance, HR, and business development all knew what I was doing in each area.

For me, that practice of sharing what I was doing three thousand miles away was a shift from operating with a "don't ask me, it's all fine, you'll know when I need you" attitude that I'd had when I worked at the headquarters office so many years prior. In the end, I probably swung too far the other way, but at least I'd popped myself out of the "high performer, loner" box I had been in.

Over the last fifteen years since I decided to stop making counteroffers to departing employees and focus on the people who were focused on their work, while at the same time telling those departing employees that they could come back, I've found that people who return to work in my organizations are happier, are more productive, and have a positive influence on the organization. They roll with the punches more easily; they can compare a bad day for us with a bad day at their previous job. "This is nothing," I've heard some returned employees say when the shit hits the fan. And they have respect and consideration from their colleagues they may not have felt before. "Now that I've been at another job at this level, I understand what disrespectful and unsupportive feels like," Wilchins told me. "It makes me want to do even more here."

# CHAPTER 9

# Creating Your Own Alumni Club
## A Blueprint

The first step in creating an environment that encourages boomeranging at any level—whether that is fostering advocates for the company, converting clients, or promoting a climate that persuades former employees to return—is maintaining a formal tie to your former employees. LinkedIn is populated with thousands of corporate alumni clubs administered by former employees; this is not what I'm talking about. I'm talking about a company-directed alumni effort with the purpose of reinforcing former employees' time at your company. Keep people up to date with what they contributed to; maintain your company as part of each former employee's identity; keep providing value to your former employees.

Why? Talent, talent, talent. Oh, and some business, too.

The Boomerang Principle starts with an open mind-set and is powered by a corporate alumni program.

The fight for talent never wanes; in good economies or bad, the best people are always in demand. Your company's ability to create advocates who refer candidates, recommend you as an employer, and reinforce the value of being an employee at your organization will increasingly be a strategic measure in business. When you keep helping your employees after they leave you, you will have an advantage in recruiting. In an increasingly connected world, we are all maintaining dozens of communication and information webs that we influence and which, in turn, influence us. Being present in our former employees' information webs can be a low-effort, short-term investment that yields tremendous long-term benefits.

## The Gold Standard

McKinsey & Co. operates a sophisticated alumni program that I repeatedly heard referred to as the gold standard as I was conducting my research. The large department has been led for almost ten years by Sean Brown, global director of alumni relations and a McKinsey alum who turned around the alumni program of MIT's Sloan Management School of Business between 2003 and 2007. Brown has created at McKinsey an alumni program that permeates the company at every level, with a proprietary web platform that operates a robust professional network for alumni as well as newsletters, job boards, events, and an active education/information program that each month hosts multiple strategic alumni-only webinars, which regularly attract hundreds of participants.

While business development is clearly a by-product of a strong talent brand and the company's alumni program, success for McKinsey's program is measured by enrollment, engagement (attendance at events and/or webinars, newsletter open rates, etc.), and recruiting success. "It's 100 percent about the people," says Brown. "One-hundred percent about helping others be their best."

In fact, in a study measuring the influence of different formal, informal, owned, and platform-driven communities, people looking or being recruited for work "trust the voice of your alumni more than LinkedIn, Glassdoor, or Facebook."[1] Owning your own process and creating your own platform—automated or not—will be the single more important thing companies of any size can do to improve their bottom line. According to research by Boston Consulting Group, LinkedIn, and Conenza Research, improving a corporate talent brand through a robust alumni community yields "40% higher retention, 50% more applicants, 50% savings in recruiting" and an amazing 2.4 multiple in revenue growth.[2]

Boomerangs need not return to your organization as employees to be effective, loyal, and valuable allies.

Microsoft, McKinsey, SAP, PwC, and others are dedicated to creating alumni networks for medium to large to very large companies—from one thousand to more than one hundred thousand alumni. Some companies, including global management consulting firm McKinsey, have created their own systems or their own alumni platforms, while others have created tailored modules within Salesforce, SAP, or other CRM systems, and a small handful of companies, such as Conenza, have created software solutions specifically for company-based alumni platforms.

All of these systems are built to in some way automate or facilitate communication, create community among former employees, and integrate with internal systems. "The key is to be able to automate as much as possible from the work that happens anyway in the business," said James Sinclair, principal of EnterpriseJungle, an SAP partner that co-created SAP's alumni management solution for SAP-native and non-native environments.

## The Power of Alumni

The power of an alumni system has been made immediately tangible for one of Sinclair's clients. Once the module was deployed, the client was able to query over five thousand of its alumni. One of the stunning results was that the client discovered that 74 percent of the company's alumni would be willing to be recruited by the company for future positions.

"This was astonishing. I don't think most HR departments would have even thought to ask former employees before—and here 74 percent of their alumni were willing to be recruited! It was a real 'holy crap' moment," said Sinclair, excitedly.

Microsoft's alumni program was started in 1995 by a former employee who, after seven years at the company, found that he missed the easy relationship building inherent to in-house company positions. After a lukewarm greenlight from Microsoft's CEO and COO, Tony Audino started the Microsoft Alumni Network (MSA), one of the first formal corporate alumni networks, with a goal "to maintain the strong personal, professional relationships so many people make inside Microsoft." Audino continued, "I just believed everyone would benefit if we could stay together to share our stories and insights, collaborate and stay engaged with each other." While initial reception for the network from Microsoft's leadership was tepid, the company now fully embraces the power of the community. As one Microsoft alumni shared with me, "It's always been good to be from Microsoft, but with the alumni network, it's invaluable." Eleven years after starting Microsoft's network, Audino founded Conenza, an independent company that builds and manages corporate alumni communities around the world.

SAP, the worldwide enterprise software application company headquartered in Germany, has seen dramatic results after less than a year of initiating a global alumni program. Margret Klein-Magar, global vice president and head of SAP alumni relations, a relatively new responsibility, was inspired to fully develop SAP's alumni program after a dinner conversation she had with a former employee who had been part of SAP's Early Tenant program, a cooperative program with Germany's Cooperative State University which combines on-the-job training with academic study. The young woman Klein-Magar spoke with had, after graduating, moved to the United States to attend business school in Chicago and had then been hired by McKinsey. During the dinner, the former SAP employee shared with Klein-Magar that McKinsey employees are valued as alumni from day one. "I love SAP, but at McKinsey I am always up to date with what's going on at the company and with former employees." Klein-Magar immediately keyed in on her former colleague's comments.

Shortly thereafter, Klein-Magar presented the idea of the SAP alumni program to other senior management and was immediately given the green light to lead the group. As of August 2016, the SAP program has focused on three initiatives:

1. Integrating the alumni program with SAP's company-wide customer relationship management system to glean relevant information already in circulation so the alumni team can tailor existing content for its alumni audience
2. Enrolling former SAP employees into the SAP alumni community so they are able to connect and provide a valuable community platform for fellow alumni
3. Hosting high-profile "key suite" events that bring together SAP alumni who currently hold high-level strategic positions at other companies

So far, results have been amazing, according to Klein-Magar. "What we've learned is that our alumni want to be connected to us more formally," she said. "They are already our brand ambassadors, which I think we knew, but we didn't fully appreciate the extent to which many of our former employees go out of their way to extend our brand. Now, by keeping them informed and by bringing them together, we see more tangible examples of how important the alumni network is. When we help our alumni do their business, they win and we win."

In order to implement SAP's alumni program, Klein-Magar has put together a cross-functional team across several different departments, including marketing, communications, customer service, and sales, as well as local ambassadors responsible for alumni activities in each region in which SAP operates around the world. On average, people assigned to this team spend about 20 percent of their time on alumni program-related activities. "It's early days in our alumni program, but we are confident that this effort will more than pay off for SAP," Klein-Magar said.

How will SAP measure success in its alumni program? Through three key metrics:

1. Growth in the network; once the system was deployed, more than five thousand alumni enrolled, and SAP aims to double and triple that number over the next several years.
2. Business development opportunities and wins trackable to alumni.
3. Rehiring rate of early tenants, interns, and other former employees.

Klein-Magar emphasizes the importance of CEO and senior management endorsement and involvement to the success of the program: "Our alumni are CEOs, CIOs, CMOs, and COOs of significant companies around the world. We could never capture their attention if our senior team was not fully involved with our program."

While large companies with thousands or tens of thousands of employees and alumni can show large numbers to quantify the return on investment of deploying a third-party or customized system, smaller companies can experience the same proportional return on an alumni program; not having lots of people or other resources to devote to the effort is not an excuse to delay starting an alumni program at smaller companies. Small companies with fewer than one hundred employees and medium-sized companies with fewer than one thousand employees (it's all in what is big to you) don't have the engines that will generate the big numbers for an externally impressive report. However, the percentage of return for small and medium-sized companies is, by definition, higher as a percentage of revenue than it is for companies with $100 million to $15 billion in revenue. So, even if smaller organizations can't dedicate megabucks to a customized solution, they can still realize the advantages of an alumni program in their business. No matter the size of your company or your alumni cohort, every organization can and should create a network platform for its alumni.

As Reid Hoffman, cofounder and chairman of LinkedIn, wrote in his book *The Alliance*, "Establishing a corporate alumni network, which requires relatively little investment, is the next logical step in maintaining a relationship of mutual trust, mutual investment, and mutual benefit in an era where lifetime employment is no longer the norm."[3]

## A Blueprint for a Valuable Alumni Program

Those who run large corporate alumni programs have ample advice for companies of all sizes that are starting their own programs. "Keep it simple and start small," advises SAP's Klein-Magar. "Listen to what your alumni tell you they want from the company and the program and do what you can to provide it. Find them and then keep in touch with them." Your program does not need to have a lot of bells and whistles to be effective, it simply needs to be valuable to the people you seek to stay connected to. Following are fundamental elements of an alumni program:

**Objective: Maintain strong relationships with former employees.**

**Strategies**
- Create a vibrant, valuable community of former employees.
- Share valuable information that helps former employees in their professional development.
- Keep former employees up to date on company performance, services, products, and achievements.
- Showcase achievements of corporate alumni.
- Surprise and delight loyal former employees with small gifts, discounts, or other perks.

In Conenza's benchmarking study of formal and information alumni programs between 2014 and 2015, corporate alumni ranked the following network benefits in terms of popularity:

- Networking opportunities (45 percent)
- Job opportunities

- Alumni stories
- Exclusive perks and discounts
- Special events
- Access to company news and information
- Career development and services (10 percent)

## Create a Community for Your Alumni

If your company doesn't have the resources to devote to creating and deploying its own private social network, consider using private Facebook groups or LinkedIn groups.

- **Facebook groups.** Private Facebook groups have become very powerful affinity groups, and are effective with Boomers, Gen Xers, and Millennials. Of course, your Facebook group is only as strong as the number of your former employees who are active on Facebook. The goal of the Facebook group is to help former employees stay connected to your organization and keep current with what's going on. Post at least weekly into the Facebook group with a range of information, including news, blog posts, pictures of work events, and so forth. Any communication plan will be significantly helped by a well-administered private Facebook group, but don't count on the Facebook group as your only communication vehicle.
- **LinkedIn groups.** LinkedIn is littered with thousands of unofficial alumni groups administered by former employees. Very few of these groups are effective as strong communication vehicles from companies to their former employees, given that the valuable groups are the ones that have a high ratio of active participants. When you publish a blog post, posting the link into a LinkedIn group does help distribute the information further. However, do not rely on LinkedIn as the host of your alumni communication experience.
- **Directory of former employees.** While a "social" community is key to creating a vibrant dynamic among corporate alumni, the

asset most alumni asked for is a directory of former employees. This is also the most valuable asset for your company, so creating and sharing it privately is a win-win. Of course, the larger and older the company, the more valuable the directory will be. If your company has more than a hundred alumni, consider creating a web-based private directory that allows former employees to maintain profiles and search other alumni for partners and/or employees. The benefit, of course, is that you will have a current database of your former employees that you can tap for recruiting or partnering. The second benefit is less measurable, but those companies that provide this level of extra value to former employees will likely experience higher loyalty from those employees, which means less poaching.

When employees and alumni feel tied to their former employers, it is rare for them to take current employees with them when they leave or to come back and poach current employees later.

## Sharing Information

Keeping people in your fold depends upon regular, valuable communication that informs, helps, and celebrates your former employees. Throughout your organization, you most likely have ample information that is relevant and helpful for former employees—if it's useful for current employees, it's probably useful for former employees. Of course, you need not put as much effort into sharing and bringing training material to life for your former employees, but sharing most of the information you have is a low-cost, low-effort activity that helps extend your reach and impact, reinforce your culture, and strengthen your employee value proposition.

Consider sharing the following:

- **Training and development materials.** Do you provide management training for new managers? Create a public version, complete with your formatting and logos, and provide it online for download. Valuable topics range from leadership to delegation, conflict resolution to personality-driven communication, leveraging strengths to expectation setting, effective speaking to high value meetings, moving from individual contributor to first-time manager, project management to sprint planning, and command and control versus coaching leadership. You have lots of shareable material that helps you create your special sauce, and sharing this will not compromise your competitive edge.

- **Market updates.** As you keep your staff up to date on the market, key global developments, demographic information, or changes in market dynamics, consider providing a public or private version to your former employees. Remove your company action items or strategic decisions before sharing. Even confining what you share to general topics such as generational differences in the workplace, new communication platforms, shifting demographics, smartphone usage patterns, education trends or purchasing trends, and the like can be tremendously helpful.

- **Book club recommendations.** Are you recommending specific books to your staff or providing training based on books? Share the recommendation and a brief review of why the book is important to your organization. Did you make a bulk order at a discount? Consider offering former employees a discounted copy. Or send your top twenty alumni a copy of the book with a personal note.

- **Mentor programs.** One of the most valuable things a corporate alumni program can do is provide a structure that enables positive mentoring relationships among its alumni. Indeed, my research confirmed that the number one request Millennial employees have is for a mentor. This can be tricky, as, in general, people seek mentors at the highest level of the value chain, which becomes unsustainable quickly. However, as EnterpriseJungle's Sinclair found in some of their pilot programs, connecting younger alumni with retired alumni has been extremely valuable to the mentor (retired), the mentee, and the company. "Mentorship is incredibly valuable for today's workforce, and if they can get great mentors through the alumni network, then you've created an even strong relationship with them," said Sinclair. Organizations that provide mentoring to current and former employees will be more valuable than those that don't.

There are many information distribution options you can put in place that create different levels of ease of use, connection, or branding, depending on the size of your alumni group:

- **Your own website.** From a branding, affiliation point of view, the strongest position is creating a password-protected website specifically for your former employees and putting the shareable information behind a password. This requires dedicated manpower and a commitment to long-term alumni development. Several of the established management consulting firms maintain proprietary websites for their former employees, from which they publish blogs, host webinars, and share material with logins.
  Even if you don't have the resources to dedicate to a private alumni web presence, there are many other options that are simple for both the users (former employees) and the administrators (current employees).

- **Cloud-based storage utilities.** Dropbox, Box, SugarSync, and Google Drive are just four of the many cloud-based sharing platforms that can be easily configured to share documents with former employees. If you use this type of sharing mechanism, make sure that you lock down documents so that they are read only and cannot be edited by anyone but those authorized. Keep employee and former employee folders separate. For the best control, use the professional or business versions of these solutions, which involve a small fee.

- **SlideShare.** Owned by LinkedIn, SlideShare is a popular knowledge-sharing platform on which you can upload presentations, infographics, documents, or videos for private or public sharing. As a content uploader, you can create a profile page and regularly share your content on the platform. LinkedIn's search function allows anyone to find your information. By establishing a regular content profile and consistently sharing the links to your different content by embedding them in e-mail, blog posts, or social media posts, you'll be able to easily share your material with your former employees and use the channel to establish your company as a knowledge sharer among a much broader audience.

## Keep Former Employees Up to Date on Products, Services, and News

The low-hanging fruit in the communication flow to former employees is information about company products, services, and milestones. However, a small amount of effort will go a long way toward helping your former employees feel more in the know than your target audience. Instead of folding your alumni into your general information push, separate them and send them a specific e-mail with an appropriate introduction and closing. If you are offering webinars to introduce new products, hold one specifically for former employees. If it's appropriate for your product or service, offer a former-employee discount—perhaps half of the discount your employees receive. Including former employees in any "friends and family" discounts will help you create and maintain allegiance to the company and its brands.

Following are useful vehicles for communicating with your alumni:

- **E-mail.** E-mail is the most direct, easiest to control, and most readily personalized communication vehicle for reaching former employees. I recommend using a web-based e-mail platform for alumni communications so that you can measure open rates, leverage assets with other e-mail campaigns, and keep track of your annual communications. Many e-mail platforms have different service levels at different cost levels. Consider MailChimp, Emma, and Constant Contact for entry-level systems that you can grow with. If you want more options, control, and flexibility and are willing to dedicate more resources to getting the most out of the platform, consider InfusionSoft or AWeber.

- **CRM (customer relationship management).** Depending on who is managing former employee communications at your company, you may consider using an implemented CRM system such as Hubspot, Marketo, or Salesforce to manage alumni communications; however, these full-function systems require significant training and customization if you want to leverage them fully. If the person responsible for these communications doesn't usually use these systems, I recommend going with a lower-end platform.

- **Blog.** If your company has a blog, consider adding your former employees to the subscription list. Make sure they can opt out if they don't wish to receive blog updates via e-mail.

- **Snail mail.** If your alumni group is fewer than one hundred people and you are confident that you have accurate contact information, use regular mail once or twice a year with appropriate notes or information. Consider sending birthday cards to former employees during their birth month. If your company sends a holiday or end-of-the-year card, add your former employees to your mailing list. As you hear about former employees' achievements or life milestones, send a note of congratulations. In our digital world, paper stands out, and the little bit of extra effort it takes to write a card and put it in the mail makes an impact.

## Celebrate Your Alumni

Showcasing your former employees achievements is part of the symbiotic relationship between your company and your alumni. By holding up these successes in newsletters or posts into private social networks, the company honors the former colleague and implicitly attaches itself to the achievement. For current employees, this reinforces the value of the experience they are getting through their own tenures at the company, and demonstrates a commitment to honoring individual contribution over the long run; its impossible to quantify the value of this except to say "big."

Simple ways to celebrate these milestones include:

1. sharing alumni news on company social platforms (open or private)
2. interviewing the former employee about their achievement and for a short profile in the alumni newsletter.
3. Sending a handwritten note to the former employee congratulating them on their achievement.

## Surprise and Delight

Earlier, I outlined how to show appreciation for current employees by honoring their contributions and celebrating their achievements and life milestones. These efforts range from no-cost recognition to cash bonuses. It's important to ensure that the cash value of anything you send to former employees is outweighed by what your current employees can receive. If you're not doing something like this for your current employees, do not pursue a surprise and delight (S&D) program for your former employees.

> Surprise and delight (verb): to pleasantly amaze a person with an act, gesture, or gift that makes the recipient feel special and valued

The easiest way to make surprise and delight part of your former-employee program is to incorporate your former employees into the S&D program your marketing or communications team is executing now. Usually, this includes following former employees on social media platforms such as Instagram, Twitter, Facebook, or Snapchat. For instance, if your marketing includes offering discounts and coupons on social media, follow your former employees on Instagram, Twitter, or Snapchat and direct message them with coupons or promotions if they are following the company back.

If you are a product company and your product can support a former employee in her personal goals, consider sending an S&D care package before a big event. For example, send protein or energy bars, apparel, water bottles, or other gadgets to someone who is participating in a race on land or water. If you have a personal care company, send appropriate care packages to former employees who follow your company on social media before a life milestone, perhaps when a former employee becomes a parent or his child goes to college.

When you get swag for your employees—T-shirts, water bottles, USBs, umbrellas, beach chairs, and so on—consider adding to the order so you can send items to a subset of your former employees. If you have a large group of alumni, you might allow them to enter a raffle to win swag, or have the first twenty responders to send an e-mail receive the item.

While a surprise and delight campaign usually has a measurement target for social share (percentage of people who are gifted who then share a picture of the gift and a thank you on social media), the motivation and KPI for former employees should be adjusted. The goal is to delight your former employee by remembering them or by providing an added benefit for having once been employed by the company. Any social sharing is an added benefit. At the same time, you can increase the likelihood of social sharing by using the social media filter (who follows the company on your social media channels) for the alumni group.

## The Ultimate Surprise and Delight

In the late '90s I was vice president of communications at SEGA of America. During that time, SEGA created a new company, SEGASoft, by spinning off a large group of its software developers and producers. Nobuo Mii was brought in to become the CEO of SEGASoft; he left IBM in the middle of the performance year to join the company. One day, about six months into his tenure, my scheduled meeting with Mr. Mii got sidetracked at the beginning as he shared with me that IBM had just sent him his bonus for the previous year, even though they technically didn't have to. "This is what great companies do," I remember him telling me. "They honor the people who helped them even when they leave." He was visibly moved by IBM's loyalty to him. That image has had as big an impact as any other in forming my own philosophy about lifetime employee loyalty.

## How Often to Communicate

A healthy alumni communication program can range in frequency from twice a week to once a quarter depending on the size and nature of the group, what you provide, and how you provide those touch points. If you're just starting, plan on quarterly communication via e-mail as a starting point. "Cadence is important," says Conenza's Audino. "Decide on the engagement strategy and frequency of different activities, and stick to it."

If you have a weekly or monthly CEO e-mail that could be external facing, add your former employees to this e-mail list with an introduction explaining that you've added them and how they can unsubscribe.

To maintain a robust alumni offering—including webinars, online directories, and events—regular monthly e-mail communication is critical.

### A Little Inspiration Goes a Long Way

Robert Glazer, the CEO of Acceleration Partners, an Inc. 500 affiliate and digital marketing agency, sends a weekly Friday Forward "inspiration" e-mail to his employees, partners, and friends. In 2016, he opened this distribution up to friends and clients. Every week he shares what's on his mind as a leader of his organization; topics range from how to respond to national events, books he's found useful, service behavior reminders, or articles or interviews he found particularly helpful. Each e-mail ends with an inspirational quote. This short e-mail—fewer than five hundred words—shows up reliably in my e-mail every Friday morning. And whenever I'm asked for a referral for digital marketing services, Acceleration Partners is at the top of my list. He's cut through the competitors vying for a piece of our clients, first by providing great service and, second, by continually being useful to me as a leader of my own business. You can sign up for Glazer's e-mail on www.fridayfwd.com.

Blend e-mail, online events, snail mail, and social media to offer multiple touch points. Just as with any communication program, creating a varied program that meets people where they are is critical for maximum impact. Given that the goal is to maintain strong relationships with your former employees, regardless of their age or the region in which they live, the most effective program will most likely include at least quarterly e-mail, weekly or biweekly social media posting, and annual snail mail. The blend of touchpoints needs to be relevant to the alumni base and the content you have to share. Sophisticated corporate alumni programs such as that run by McKinsey don't use third-party social media platforms; rather, they rely on their proprietary online systems to create the multiple touch points for their worldwide alumni.

Regardless of the frequency with which you communicate, the quality of the writing and the usefulness of the information are paramount.

An e-mail schedule may look something like this:

- January: Outlook on the new year
- April or May: Update on Q1
- July: Summer info break; first half market update; Q2 update
- November: Holiday greeting; annual update

In each e-mail, consider having a regular feature such as an inspirational quote, a promotional offer, and/or an information-share link to training material.

Ask for help in recruiting in every e-mail. "As you know, we are always looking for great people to join our team. Please call [name] if you are interested in hearing about the open positions or have a recommendation for us."

At a minimum, plan to e-mail your former employees on a quarterly basis.

## Helping Former Employees Through Alumni Clubs

Colleges and private schools depend on their alumni to advocate for application and matriculation, to fundraise for endowment, and ultimately for survival. Corporations not only can take a page out of the best college alumni programs, but they have the advantage of not having to ask for money in any of their communications.

| College Alumni Program | Corporate Alumni Program |
| --- | --- |
| Welcomes students to the alumni program during their tenure as students | Welcomes employees to the alumni program after employees leave the company |
| Alumni magazine highlights current student life, faculty achievements, and alumni profiles and milestones | Quarterly e-mail newsletter communicates company updates and shares information |
| Regional alumni events bring cohorts or classes together to share, serve, or learn | Annual regional meetups offer brief company update, networking opportunities (if large enough) |
| Provides exceptional travel/adventure experiences hosted by college faculty | X |
| Hosts alumni weekends annually on campus; organizes at five-year increments, seeking increasingly large class gifts | X |
| Conducts annual fundraising campaigns | X |
| Conducts capital campaigns | X |

| College Alumni Program | Corporate Alumni Program |
|---|---|
| Taps into alumni for student and alumni networking | Offers ad hoc career mentoring for former employees |
| Offers alumni education opportunities via classes, webinars, and events | Provides training and development materials, market and research information, and webinars |

## Community Events: A Page out of KQED's Playbook

With three TV stations, two radio stations, a robust and innovative digital footprint including its popular and growing web destination and a prolific streaming content profile on many platforms, KQED serves more than ten million people from Sacramento to San Francisco, Napa to San Jose, Oakland to Monterey. More than two hundred thousand people regularly support KQED as members with monetary donations from $40 to $10,000 and up. To help maintain members' ties to the station, KQED holds more than three hundred events every year—from large screenings of new programs to intimate tours of the station and meet and greets with the station's radio, television, web, and education personalities. None of these events are fundraisers; they are simply extensions of the organization's mission to support lifelong learning and help increase members' allegiance to the station.

## Who Is Responsible for an Alumni Program?

Creating and managing corporate alumni programs is a relatively new responsibility in the companies that have alumni programs, and the person or team responsible varies from company to company. Titles of those responsible for this corporate effort range from CEO to chief of staff, to HR specialist, to director of alumni program, to director of public relations or communications or VP of marketing. I recommend that this

effort live as close to the CEO as possible and within the communications department, with dotted-line collaboration with human resources.

Both Conenza's Audino and EnterpriseJungle's Sinclair agree that the
most effective corporate alumni programs reside somewhere in the marketing or communication departments and are managed as high-touch
brand ambassador programs. "While there may be a business development goal or result," says Audino, "managing the corporate alumni program from the business development department gives the impression
that the company only values its alumni for their potential to bring revenue to their former employer. Nothing stops an alumni program faster in
its track than this impression."

Search for "corporate alumni manager" positions and you'll find
everything but that; while the function has been growing over the past
eight to ten years, we are just at the beginning of institutionalizing the
function and the strategic imperative for this department.

## What Does a Great Alumni Manager Look Like?[4]

Great alumni managers are connectors, resourceful, service oriented, and
enthusiastic. They are able to leverage internal resources and assets wisely
for corporate alumni without a lot of structure or authority. They are
able to forge strong relationships among different company departments
from the CEO's office to product development, research, marketing, and
human resources and customer service in order to identify opportunities
for sharing and connecting that bring value to everyone. The person in
this role must carry the alumni flag proudly within an organization that
may or may not yet fully embrace the value of a strong alumni network.
Specific assets and skills include being a self-starter, being proficient and
prolific with social media channels, being an excellent communicator,
and being able to get things done.

Alumni program manager function: to build and maintain relationships with employees and alumni for a mutually beneficial

alliance that keeps former employees close to the company and creates opportunities and rewards for company advocacy

Based on its experience, Conenza recommends that alumni community managers be resourceful, service-oriented, and demonstrated connectors; experienced in academic or corporate alumni program management or community management; and have a strong interest and ability in social media implementation.

"The most successful alumni program managers are collaborators, with strong relationship-building skills, with have a very positive outlook, and who do what it takes to bring information and people from all over the organization to bear for their audience—the alumni," advises Audino. "You've got to have someone who is flexible and who wants to deliver value and who is genuinely enthusiastic about the company."

As much as job descriptions and audience responsibilities have shifted dramatically in the past five years among people responsible for communications within companies and between companies and their stakeholders, pinning an exact job description that will stay static for a long time is folly. Better to find a person who fits Audino's description and build a position around that person. As long as what you want to measure—engagement, attendance, leads, and so on—is very clear from the beginning, get started, even if your description is not perfect.

While corporate alumni programs have been around for more than a decade, they have, for the most part, flown under the radar. We are at an inflection point today, and those companies that put in the apparatus to retain relationships with their former employees with a corporate alumni program will benefit most from the Boomerang Principle.

The Boomerang Principle starts with intention and is powered by a corporate alumni program.

# CONCLUSION

# Putting It All Together So Your Alumni Boomerang Back to You

Those companies that allow and encourage their former employees to return will always have a strategic advantage over those that don't. Why? Because those boomerang-friendly companies will be focused on ensuring the most positive, high-producing work environments possible, knowing that they are fostering lifelong advocates who will be valuable long after they leave the company.

Talented employees, cognizant of ensuring their personal brands are relevant and interesting, will seek to return to former employers when the opportunity and time are right, confident that multiple tours of duty will be viewed as positive by the people who matter to their careers.

Millennials, and the Generation Zs coming up behind them, know they have much longer careers ahead of them than their parents planned for, and these young people are determined to forge lives that allow them to honor their values and the purposes they feel so deeply. To attract the best of this younger talent, companies must focus on those things that make their environments good for their employees while they work there and not worry about how their tenure might be, confident in the knowledge that the value of an employee need not end when the paychecks stop. Companies of all sizes should look first in their alumni pool for the best candidates when they have open positions.

Management: Stop lamenting what feels like broken loyalty in short-term employees. If you're holding onto the past, you're hurting your company and your own opportunities. Build a culture of value that consistently greens your own pastures. Nurture your alumni, helping them to realize their goals after they leave the company; be confident that your alumni, well nurtured, will provide the company many dividends over time.

Employees: Keep your own goals front and center as you navigate your careers through the many vagaries the American economy will go through in the coming years. Don't leave a job just to leave a job; leave a job to go to a better one, one that advances your career, or at least where you think you want your career to go. Know that your career will have many stops—up the ladder, across the trellis, and down a step every once in a while. Keep moving forward no matter the step or stop.

The beautiful thing about a boomerang is that it can travel long and high and return to where it started. The path it takes can be wide and long, depending on how well (or with how much force) it is thrown into the air. The area it covers is large and varied; the footprint a boomerang makes in each throw is valuable.

Now is the time for companies to embrace the value of the boomerang path, which gathers speed and area while it returns and is all the more valuable because it can be deployed again.

# Notes

## Introduction

1. Peter Belmi and Jeffrey Pfeffer, "How 'Organization' Can Weaken the Norm of Reciprocity," *Academy of Management Discoveries* 1.1 (2015): 93–113.
2. Eilene Zimmerman, "Jeffrey Pfeffer: Why Companies No Longer Reward Loyal Employees," *Insights by Stanford Business*, February 20, 2015, https://www.gsb.stanford.edu/insights/jeffrey-pfeffer-why-companies-no-longer-reward-loyal-employees.
3. D'Vera Cohn, "A Demographic Portrait of the Millennial Generation," *Pew Research Center Social & Demographic Trends*, last modified February 24, 2010, http://www.pewsocialtrends.org/2010/02/24/a-demographic-portrait-of-the-millennial-generation/.
4. Workplace Trends, "The Corporate Culture and Boomerang Employee Study," last modified September 1, 2015, https://workplacetrends.com/the-corporate-culture-and-boomerang-employee-study/.
5. Lee Caraher, *Millennials & Management* (Boston: Bibliomotion, 2014).
6. Workplace Trends, "The Corporate Culture and Boomerang Employee Study."
7. Michael Hopkins, "What Should You Say When an Employee Quits?" *Inc.*, March 1, 1998, http://www.inc.com/magazine/19980301/886.html.
8. Betsy Scuteri, "The State of Small Business in 2015," *Business*, last modified May 5, 2015, http://www.business.com/entrepreneurship/the-state-of-small-businesses-in-2015/.

## Chapter 1

1. *Merriam Webster Dictionary*, "loyalty," last accessed June 18, 2016, http://www.merriam-webster.com/dictionary/loyalty.

2.  Christopher J. Goodman and Steven M. Mance, "Employment loss and the 2007-2009 recession: an overview" Monthly Labor Review, April 2011, U.S. Department of Labor https://www.bls.gov/mlr/2011/04/art1full.pdf

3.  "Quick Facts about Student Debt," *The Institute for College Access & Success*, March, 2014 http://ticas.org/sites/default/files/pub_files/Debt_Facts_ and_Sources.pdf.

4.  U.S. Department of Labor, Bureau of Labor Statistics, "Economic News Release: Employee Tenure Summary" September 22, 2016.

5.  U.S. Department of Labor, Bureau of Labor Statistics, "Economic News Release: Employee Tenure Summary" September 22, 2016.

6.  Ray Williams, "Is Loyalty Dead?" *Psychology Today*, July 4, 2011, accessed June 4, 2016, www.psychologytoday.com/blog/wired-success/201107/is-loyalty-dead.

7.  Penelope Trunk, "Employee Loyalty Isn't Gone, It's Just Different," April 29, 2007, accessed June 4, 2016, http://blog/penelopetrunk.com/2007/29/ employee-loyalty-isnt-gone-its-just-different/.

8.  "Declining Employee Loyalty: A Casualty of the New Workplace," *Knowledge @ Wharton*, Wharton, University of Pennsylvania, http:// knowledge.wharton.upenn.edu/article/declining-employee-loyalty-a- casualty-of-the-new-workplace/.

9.  Comment posted by Grand Guigol, "Employee Loyalty Isn't Gone It's Just Different," April 29, 2007.

10. Myles Udland, "Hillary: Corporate America Is Obsessed with 'Quarterly Capitalism'—Here's How I'd Change That," *Business Insider*, April 1, 2016.

11. "Is Loyalty Dead?"

12. *The Big Short.* DVD. Directed by Adam McKay (Los Angeles: Paramount Pictures, 2015).

13. Lawrence R. Samuel, *The American Dream: A Cultural History* (Syracuse: Syracuse UP, 2012).

14. Chris Arnade, "Who Still Believes in the American Dream?" *The Atlantic*, September 15, 2015, accessed June 4, 2016, http://www.theatlantic.com/ business/archive/2015/09/american-dreams-portraits/.

15. Don Penn and Mark Penn "The American Dream: Personal Optimists, National Pessimists," *The Atlantic*, July 1, 2015, accessed June 27, 2016, http://www. theatlantic.com/national/archive/2015/07/aspen-ideas-american-dream- survey/397274/.

16. "5 Reasons Why You Should Consider Wearing a Wrist Watch," *Lifehacker*, last modified September 5, 2016, http://www.lifehacker.guru/5-reasons- why-you-should-consider-wearing-a-wrist-watch/.

## Chapter 2

1.  "Declining Employee Loyalty: A Casualty of the New Workplace," May 9, 2012 Wharton School of the University of Pennsylvania, *Knowledge @ Wharton*, accessed June 18, 2016, http://www.knowledge.wharton.upenn. edu/articles/declining-employee-loyalty-a-casualty-of-the-new-workplace.

2.  Doug Horn, "The Reasons Why Workplace Loyalty Is Declining" *Recruitifi*, January 21, 2015, accessed June 18, 2016, http://www.blog.recruitifi.com/ the-reasons-why-workplace-loyalthy-is-declining.

3.  Nikelle Murphy, "Your Employer Is Not Your Friend and Young People Know It," *Cheat Sheet*, May 16, 2016, accessed June 18, 2016, http://www. cheatsheet.com/money-career/your-employer-isn't-your-friend-and-millen nials-know-it.html.

4.  Shawn Murphy, "Work That Matters Podcast 21," *podcast audio*, Leading and Working with Millennial Employees with Lee Caraher, MP3, accessed March 19, 2015, https://itunes.apple.com/us/podcast/work-that-matters-podcast/id741665948?mt=2.

5.  Nikelle Murphy, "Your Employer Is Not Your Friend and Young People Know It," *Cheat Sheet*, May 16, 2016, accessed June 18, 2016, http:// www.cheatsheet.com/money-career/your-employer-isn't-your-friend-and-millennials-know-it.html.

6.  Dharmesh Shah, "7 Qualities of a Truly Loyal Employee," *LinkedIn*, July 13, 2013, accessed June 4, 2016, http://www.linkedin.com/ pulse/20130723130110–6558789–7-qualities-of-a-truly-loyal-employee.

7.  "Culture Code: Creating a Lovable Company," *Hubspot* (2013).

8.  Dan Lyons, *Disrupted: My Misadventure in the Start-Up Bubble* (New York: Hachette, 2016).

9.  Lauren Holiday, "Working for This Startup Wasn't Hell—You're Just Old," *Fortune*, March 30, 2016, http://www.fortune.com/2016/03/30/ hubspot-startup-dan-lyons/.

10. Dawn Rasmussen, "Loyalty: A Dead Workplace Value?" *Careerealism*, September 6, 2011, accessed June 4, 2016, http://www.careerealism.com/ building-workplace-loyalty.

11. Oprah Winfrey, "Winfrey's Commencement Address," *Harvard Gazette*, May 31, 2013, http://news.harvard.edu/gazette/story/2013/05/winfreys-com mencement-address/.

12. "Definition of Gig Economy," *Whatis.com*, whatis.techtarget.com/definition/ gig-economy.

13. Intuit 2020, "Report: Twenty Trends That Will Shape the Next Decade Intuit," October 2010, accessed June 4, 2016, https://http-download.intuit.com/http.intuit/CMO/intuit/futureofsmallbusiness/intuit_2020_report.pdf.

14. Jacgues Bughin, James Manyika, and Jonathan Woetzel, *Independent Work: Choice, Necessity and the Gig Economy* (New York: The McKinsey Global Institute, October 2016).

15. Jacgues Bughin, James Manyika, and Jonathan Woetzel, Independent Work: Choice, Necessity and the Gig Economy (New York: The McKinsey Global Institute, October 2016)

16. Jacgues Bughin, James Manyika, and Jonathan Woetzel, Independent Work: Choice, Necessity and the Gig Economy (New York: The McKinsey Global Institute, October 2016)

## Chapter 3

1. Tom Peters, "The Brand Called You," *Fast Company*, August 31, 1997, https://www.fastcompany.com/28905/brand-called-you.

2. "Multiple Generations @ Work," *Future Workplace LLC*, 2012, http://futureworkplace.com/wp-content/uploads/MultipleGenAtWork_infographic.pdf.

3. Tallulah David, "15 Employer Branding Stats Every HR Pro Must Know," *CareerArc.com*, no publish date given, http://www.careerarc.com/blog/2015/09/15-employer-branding-stats-every-hr-pro-must-know/.

4. David, "15 Employer Branding Stats Every HR Pro Must Know."

## Chapter 4

1. Deloitte, *2016 Deloitte Millennial Survey* (New York: Deloitte, 2016), 11.

2. Deloitte, *2016 Deloitte Millennial Survey*, 11.

3. Patrick Lencioni, *The Advantage* (San Francisco: Jossey-Bass, 2012), 91.

4. Lencioni, *The Advantage*, 91.

5. Lencioni, *The Advantage*, 91.

6. Lee Caraher, *Millennials & Management* (Boston: Bibliomotion, 2014).

7. Sarah Green "The Big Benefits of a Little Thanks," HBR IdeaCast, Episode 380, November 27, 2013 https://hbr.org/2013/11/the-big-benefits-of-a-little-thanks.

8. "The Big Benefits of a Little Thanks."

9. Deloitte, *2016 Deloitte Millennial Survey*, 6.

10. John Eades, "Why Modern Leadership Is So Hard," *LinkedIn*, August 16, 2016. https://www.linkedin.com/pulse/why-modern-leadership-so-hard-john-eades.

11. Laci Loew and Karen O'Leonard, "Leadership Development Fact-book 2012: Benchmarks and Trends in US Leadership Development," *Bersin by Deloitte*, July 2012, http://www.bersin.com/Practice/List.aspx?t=Factbook&p=leadership-development.

12. Caraher, *Millennials & Management*, 171.

## Chapter 5

1. "How College Students Think They Are More Special Than Ever," last modified January 7, 2013, http://www.dailymail.co.uk/news/article-2257715/Study-shows-college-students-think-theyre-special-read-write-barely-study.html.

2. "Everyone Thinks They Are above Average," February 7, 2013, Live Science.com http://www.cbsnews.com/news/everyone-thinks-they-are-above-average/.

3. Richard Fy, *For First Time in Modern Era, Living with Parents Edges Out Other Living Arrangements* (New York: Pew Research, 2016).

4. Allen Brizee, "Searching the WorldWideWeb: Overview, Dana Lynn Driscoll, Caitlan Spronk," OWL at Purdue https://owl.english.purdue.edu.

5. Deloitte, *2016 Deloitte Millennial Survey*.

6. Stacey Patton, "Student Evaluations: Feared, Loathed, and Not Going Anywhere," *Vitae*, May 19, 2015, www.chroniclevitae.com.

7. State Street Global Advisors, referenced in "Why Millennials Have No Problem Quitting Their Jobs," *Reuters*, January 29, 2016.

8. Deloitte referenced in "Why Millennials Have No Problem Quitting Their Jobs," *Reuters*, January 29, 2016. http://www.reuters.com/article/us-column-rebell-millennialjobs-idUSKCN0V71X6

9. "2012 HR Beat: A Survey on the Pulse of Today's Global Workforce," *SuccessFactors*, San Francisco, 2012.

10. Isha Aran, "More Than Half of Millennials Say They're Best Friends with Their Parents," *Fusion.net*, February 6, 2015.

11. "Deloitte Announces 16 Weeks of Fully Paid Family Leave Time for Caregiving," *Deloitte Press Release*, September 8, 2016, Deloitte.com.

12. Romain Hatchuel, "The Myth about Money Managers and Divorce," *The Wall Street Journal*, March 25, 2015, http://www.wsj.com/articles/romain-hatchuel-the-myth-about-money-managers-and-divorce-1427324662.

13. Shankar Vedantam, "How Money Manager's Personal Lives Affect Your Investments," *NPR*, March 24, 2015, http://www.npr.org/2015/03/24/395001579/how-money-managers-personal-lives-affect-your-investments.

14. Martin Swilling, "How to Increase Productivity by Employee Happiness," *Forbes*, December 2, 2014.
15. Merriam-Webster's Learner's Dictionary., s.v. "happy" accessed September 26, 2016, http://learnersdictionary.com/definition/happy
16. Ralph Dandrea, *The Commitment Conversation*, Paper available at ITX Corporation, Social Science Research Network http://papers.ssrn.com/sol3/papers.cfm?abstract_id=1908918.

## Chapter 6

1. "Top Attractors: Where Professionals Want to Work Now," *LinkedIn*, July 24, 2016, accessed July 24, 2016, http://lists.linkedin.com/2016/top-attractors/en/us.
2. Vivian Giang, "She Created Netflix's Culture and it Ultimately Got Her Fired" *Fast Company*, February 2, 2016, accessed July 24, 2016, https://www.fastcompany.com/3056662/the-future-of-work/she-created-netflixs-culture-and-it-ultimately-got-her-fired
3. Reed Hastings, "Netflix Culture: Freedom & Responsibility" *SlideShare*, August 1, 2009, accessed July 24, 2016, http://www.slideshare.net/reed2001/culture-1798664
4. Reed Hastings, "Netflix Culture: Freedom & Responsibility", August 1, 2009, Slideshare.net, accessed July 24, 2016, http://www.slideshare.net/reed2001/culture-1798664, page 22.
5. Reed Hastings, "Netflix Culture: Freedom & Responsibility" August 1, 2009, Slideshare.net, accessed July 24, 2016, http://www.slideshare.net/reed2001/culture-1798664, page 23.
6. Reed Hastings, "Netflix Culture: Freedom & Responsibility" Slideshare.net August 1, 2009, accessed July 24, 2016, http://www.slideshare.net/reed2001/culture-1798664, page 31.
7. Rachel Martin, "How the Architech of Netflix's Innovative Culture Lost Her Job to the System," *NPR: Planet Money*, audio recording, September 3, 2015, http://www.npr.org/2015/09/03/437291792/how-the-architech-of-netflixs-innovative-culture-lost-her-job-to-the-system.
8. Steve Henn, Correspondent, "How the Architect of Netflix's Innovative Center Lost Her Job to the System," *NPR: Planet Money*, September 3, 2015.
9. Vivian Giang, "She Created Netflix's Culture, and it Ultimately Got Her Fired" *Fast Company,* February 2, 2016, accessed July 24, 2016, https://

www.fastcompany.com/3056662/the-future-of-work/she-created-netflixs-culture-and-it-ultimately-got-her-fired

10. Caroline Fairchild, Netflix Redefined American Company Culture. Will it do the Same Abroad? CNBC.com, June 20, 2016, accessed July 24, 2016, http://www.cnbc.com/2016/06/20/netflix-redefined-american-company-culture-will-it-do-the-same-abroad.html

## Chapter 7

1. Sue Shellenbarger, "How to Leave Your Job Gracefully," *The Wall Street Journal*, August 18, 2015, http://www.wsj.com/articles/leave-your-job-gracefully-1439924165.

## Chapter 8

1. Erik Charles, "Welcoming Home the Boomerang Employee," www.xactlycorp.com/blog March 8, 2016, https://www.xactlycorp.com/blog/welcoming-home-the-boomerang-employee/#.

2. Vicki Salemi, Monster Career Expert, "The Best Job Search Strategy You're Probably Overlooking," *Monster.com blog*, http://www.monster.com/career-advice/article/best-job-search-strategy-you-are-overlooking.

3. "They're Back! New Survey Reveals Changing Mindset about Boomerang Employees and the Organizations They Once Left," *The Workforce Institute at Kronos*, September 1, 2015, http://www.kronos.com/pr/boomerang-employees-and-the-organizations-they-once-left.aspx.

4. Ellen Choy, "Boomerang Employees Are Rising in Popularity," *TheStreet.com*, April 6, 2016, accessed April 7, 2016, https://www.thestreet.com/story/13520491/1/boomerang-employees-are-rising-in-popularity.html.

## Chapter 9

1. Conenza material from www.conenza.com, supplied by Tony Audino, CEO.

2. Conenza material from www.conenza.com, supplied by Tony Audino, CEO.

3. Reid Hoffman, Ben Casnocha, and Chris Yeh, *The Alliance: Managing Talent in the Networked Age* (Cambridge, MA: Harvard Business Review Press, July 8, 2014).

4. Compiled from interviews with Conenza, McKinsey, Deloitte, & SAP.

# References

Aran, Isha. "More Than Half of Millennials Say They're Best Friends with Their Parents." *Fusion.net*, February 6, 2015. http://fusion.net/ story/45063/more-than-half-of-millennials-are-best-friends-with-their-parent/.

Arnade, Chris. "Who Still Believes in the American Dream?" *The Atlantic*, September 15, 2015. Accessed June 4, 2016. http://www.theatlantic.com/business/archive/2015/09/american-dreams-portraits/.

Belmi, Peter, and Jeffrey Pfeffer. "How 'Organization' Can Weaken the Norm of Reciprocity." *Academy of Management Discoveries* 1.1 (2015): 93–113.

Bughin, Jacgues, James Manyika, and Jonathan Woetzel. *Independent Work: Choice, Necessity and the Gig Economy.* New York: The McKinsey Global Institute, October 2016.

Caraher, Lee. *Millennials & Management.* Boston: Bibliomotion, 2014.

CBS News "Everyone Thinks They are Above Average" February 7, 2013

Charles, Erik. "Welcoming Home The Boomerang Employee" Corporate Blog Post March 8, 2016 www.xactlycorp.com/blog/welcoming-home-the-boomerang-employee/#.

Choy, Ellen. "Boomerang Employees Are Rising in Popularity." *TheStreet.com*, April 6, 2016. https://www.thestreet.com/story/13520491/1/ boomerang-employees-are-rising-in-popularity.html.

Cohn, D'Vera. "A Demographic Portrait of the Millennial Generation." *Pew Research Center Social & Demographic Trends.* Last modified

February 24, 2010. http://www.pewsocialtrends.org/2010/02/24/a-demographic-portrait-of-the-millennial-generation/.

DailyMail.co.uk, "How College Students Think They Are More Special Than Ever" January 7, 2013. http://www.dailymail.co.uk/news/article-2257715/study-shows-college-students-think-theyre-special-read-write-barely-study.html

Dandrea, Ralph. "The Commitment Conversation." Paper available at ITX Corporation, Social Science Research Network: http://papers.ssrn.com/sol3/papers.cfm?abstract_id=1908918.

David, Tallulah. "15 Employer Branding Stats Every HR Pro Must Know." *CareerArc*, N.D. http://www.careerarc.com/blog/2015/09/15-employer-branding-stats-every-hr-pro-must-know/

Deloitte. *2016 Deloitte Millennial Survey.* New York: Deloitte, 2016.

Driscoll, Dana Lynn, Caitlan Spronk, and Allen Brizee. "Searching the WorldWideWeb: Overview." No Date Given. *Purdue Online Writing Lab.* https://owl.english.purdue.edu/owl/resource/558/01/

Eades, John. "Why Modern Leadership Is So Hard." *LinkedIn*, August 16, 2016. https://www.linkedin.com/pulse/why-modern-leadership-so-hard-john-eades.

Fairchild, Caroline. "Netflix Has Redefined American Company Culture. Will It Do the Same Abroad?", June 20, 2016. Accessed July 24, 2016. http://www.cnbc.com/2016/06/20/netflix-redefined-american-company-culture-will-it-do-the-same-abroad.html

Fry, Richard. "For the First Time in Modern Era, Living with Parents Edges Out Other Living Arrangements for 18- to 34-Year Olds." *Pew Research Center*, May 24, 2016. http://www.pewsocialtrends.org/2016/05/24/for-first-time-in-modern-era-living-with-parents-edges-out-other-living-arrangements-for-18-to-34-year-olds/.

Future Workplace. "Multiple Generations @ Work." *Future Workplace LLC*, 2012. http://futureworkplace.com/wp-content/uploads/MultipleGenAtWork_infographic.pdf.

Giang, Vivian. "She Created Netflix's Culture and it Ultimately Got Her Fired" *Fast Company*, February 2, 2016. Accessed July 24, 2016.

http://www.fastcompany.com/3056187/the-future-of-work/the-woman-who-created-netflix-enviable-company-culture.

Green, Sarah "The Big Benefits of a Little Thanks." HBR IdeaCast Podcast Episode 380, November 27, 2013. https://hbr.org/2013/11/the-big-benefits-of-a-little-thanks

Hastings, Reed *Netflix Culture: Freedom & Responsibility August 1, 2009*

Hatchuel, Romain. "The Myth about Money Managers and Divorce." *The Wall Street Journal*, March 25, 2015. http://www.wsj.com/articles/romain-hatchuel-the-myth-about-money-managers-and-divorce-1427324662.

Henn, Steve. "How the Architect of Netflix's Innovative Center Lost Her Job to the System." *NPR Planet Money*, September 3, 2015. http://www.npr.org/2015/09/03/437291792/how-the-architect-of-netflixs-innovative-culture-lost-her-job-to-the-system.

Hoffman, Reid, Ben Casnocha, and Chris Yeh. *The Alliance: Managing Talent in the Networked Age.* Cambridge, MA: Harvard Business Review Press, July 8, 2014.

Holiday, Lauren. "Working for This Startup Wasn't Hell—You're Just Old." *Fortune*, March 30, 2016. http://www.fortune.com/2016/03/30/hubspot-startup-dan-lyons/.

Hopkins, Michael. "What Should You Say When an Employee Quits?" *Inc.*, March 1, 1998. http://www.inc.com/magazine/19980301/886.html.

Horn, Doug. *Recruitifi*, January 21, 2015. Accessed June 18, 2016. http://www.blog.recruitifi.com/the-reasons-why-workplace-loyalty-is-declining.

Hubspot. "Culture Code: Creating a Lovable Company." *Hubspot*, March 20, 2013. http://blog.hubspot.com/blog/tabid/6307/bid/34234/The-HubSpot-Culture-Code-Creating-a-Company-We-Love.aspx#sm.00000b9x5q4xlye41tqa8lfcjg5vz.

Institute for College Access & Success. "Quick Facts about Student Debt." http://ticas.org/sites/default/files/pub_files/Debt_Facts_and_Sources.pdf.

Intuit 2020. "Report: Twenty Trends That Will Shape the Next Decade Intuit," October 2010. https://http-download.intuit.com/http.intuit/CMO/intuit/futureofsmallbusiness/intuit_2020_report.pdf

Lencioni, Patrick. *The Advantage: Why Organizational Health Trumps Everything Else In Business*. San Francisco: Jossey-Bass, 2012.

Lifehacker. "5 Reasons Why You Should Consider Wearing a Wrist Watch." *Lifehacker*. Last modified September 5, 2016. http://www.lifehacker.guru/5-reasons-why-you-should-consider-wearing-a-wrist-watch/.

LinkedIn, "Top Attactors: Where Professionals Want to Work Now" July 24, 2016 http://lists.linkedin.com/2016/top-attractors/en/us

Loew, Laci, and Karen O'Leonard. "Leadership Development Factbook 2012: Benchmarks and Trends in US Leadership Development." *Bersin by Deloitte*, July 2012. http://www.bersin.com/Practice/List.aspx?t=Factbook&p=leadership-development.

Lyons, Dan. *Disrupted: My Misadventure in the Start-Up Bubble*. New York: Hachette, 2016.

Martin, Rachel. "How the Architech of Netflix's Innovative Culture Lost Her Job to the System." *NPR: Planet Money*, September 3, 2015. http://www.npr.org/2015/09/03/437291792/how-the-architech-of-netflixs-innovative-culture-lost-her-job-to-the-system.

*Merriam Webster Dictionary*. "Loyalty," accessed June 18, 2016. http://www.merriam-webster.com/dictionary/loyalty.

Murphy, Nikelle. "Your Employer Is Not Your Friend and Young People Know It." *Cheat Sheet*, May 16, 2016. Accessed June 18, 2016. http://www.cheatsheet.com/money-career/your-employer-isn't-your-friend-and-millennials-know-it.html.

Murphy, Shawn. *Work That Matters Podcast 21*, podcast audio, Leading and Working with Millennial Employees with Lee Caraher, MP3. Accessed March 19, 2015. https://itunes.apple.com/us/podcast/work-that-matters-podcast/id741665948?mt=2.

Patton, Stacey. "Student Evaluations: Feared, Loathed and Not Going Anywhere." *Vitae*, May 19, 2015. https://chroniclevitae.com/news/1011-student-evaluations-feared-loathed-and-not-going-anywhere.

Penn, Don, and Mark Penn. "The American Dream: Personal Optimists, National Pessimists." *The Atlantic*, July 1, 2015. Accessed June 27, 2016. http://www.theatlantic.com/national/archive/2015/07/aspen-ideas-american-dream-survey/397274/.

Peters, Tom. "The Brand Called You." *Fast Company*, August 31, 1997. https://www.fastcompany.com/28905/brand-called-you.

Rasmussen, Dawn. "Loyalty: A Dead Workplace Value?" *Careerealism*, September 6, 2011. Accessed June 4, 2016. http://www.careerealism.com/building-workplace-loyalty.

Reuters "Why Millennials Have No Problem Quitting Their Jobs", January 29, 2016 http://www.reuters.com/article/us-column-rebell-millennialjobs-idUSKCN0V71X6

Salemi, Vicki. "The Best Job Search Strategy You're Probably Overlooking" Corporate Blog Post, No Date Given, www.monster.com/career-advice/article/best-job-strategy-you-are-overlooking.

Samuel, Lawrence R. *The American Dream: A Cultural History*. Syracuse, NY: Syracuse UP, 2012.

Scuteri, Betsy. "The State of Small Business in 2015." *Business*. Last modified May 5, 2015. http://www.business.com/entrepreneurship/the-state-of-small-businesses-in-2015/.

Shah, Dharmesh. "7 Qualities of a Truly Loyal Employee." *LinkedIn*, July 13, 2013. Accessed June 4, 2016. http://www.linkedin.com/pulse/20130723130110–6558789–7-qualities-of-a-truly-loyal-employee.

Shellenbarger, Sue. "How to Leave Your Job Gracefully." *The Wall Street Journal*, August 18, 2015. http://www.wsj.com/articles/leave-your-job-gracefully-1439924165.

Swilling, Martin. "How to Increase Productivity by Employee Happiness." *Forbes*, December 2, 2014. http://www.forbes.com/sites/martinzwilling/2014/12/02/how-to-squeeze-productivity-from-employee-happiness/#2e5ad1fc1de5.

Trunk, Penelope. "Employee Loyalty Isn't Gone, It's Just Different." *Penelope Trunk*, April 29, 2007. Accessed June 4, 2016. http://blog/penelopetrunk.com/2007/29/employee-loyalty-isnt-gone-its-just-different/.

Udland, Myles. "Hillary: Corporate America Is Obsessed with 'Quarterly Capitalism'—Here's How I'd Change That." *Business Insider*, April 1, 2016. http://www.businessinsider.com/hillary-clinton-quarterly-capitalism-2016-4.

U.S. Bureau of Labor. "U.S. Bureau of Labor Statistics." http://www.bls.gov.

Vedantam, Shankar. "How Money Manager's Personal Lives Affect Your Investments." *NPR*, March 24, 2015. http://www.npr.org/2015/03/24/395001579/how-money-managers-personal-lives-affect-your-investments.

Wharton School of the University of Pennsylvania. "Declining Employee Loyalty: A Casualty of the New Workplace." *Knowledge @ Wharton*, May 9, 2012. http://knowledge.wharton.upenn.edu/article/declining-employee-loyalty-a-casualty-of-the-new-workplace/.

Whatis.com sv. Gig Economy http://techtarget.com/definition/gigeconomy

Williams, Ray. "Is Loyalty Dead?" *Psychology Today*, July 4, 2011. Accessed June 4, 2016. http://www.psychologytoday.com/blog/wired-success/201107/is-loyalty-dead.

Winfrey, Oprah. "Winfrey's Commencement Address." *Harvard Gazette*, May 31, 2013. http://news.harvard.edu/gazette/story/2013/05/winfreys-commencement-address/.

The Workforce Institute. "They're Back! New Survey Reveals Changing Mindset about Boomerang Employees and the Organizations They Once Left" September 1, 2017 www.kronos.com/pr/boomerang-employees-and-the-organizations-they-once-left.aspx.

Workplace Trends. "The Corporate Culture and Boomerang Employee Study." *Workplace Trends*, September 1, 2015. https://workplacetrends.com/the-corporate-culture-and-boomerang-employee-study/.

Zimmerman, Eilene. "Jeffrey Pfeffer: Why Companies No Longer Reward Loyal Employees." *Insights by Stanford Business*. February 20, 2015. https://www.gsb.stanford.edu/insights/jeffrey-pfeffer-why-companies-no-longer-reward-loyal-employees.

# Index

# About the Author

Lee McEnany Caraher is the founder and CEO of Double Forte, a nationally recognized public relations and digital media agency based in San Francisco that works with beloved consumer, technology, and wine brands. A sought-after communication strategist, Lee is known for her practical solutions to big problems. Her first book, *Millennials & Management: The Essential Guide to Making It Work at Work*, was informed by her failure and then success at retaining Millennials at Double Forte and her work helping organizations around the country create positive intergenerational workplaces.

Lee is active in her community and sits on the board of directors or trustees of KQED Public Media, San Francisco's Grace Cathedral, and Menlo College. A graduate of Carleton College, Lee has a degree in medieval history which she finds useful every day. She lives on the San Francisco Peninsula with her husband, their sons, and Al, their blind cat.

To learn more about working with Lee
on creating  Boomerang-Ready Workplaces,
visit www.LeeCaraher.com,
follow Lee on Twitter @LeeCaraher,
and on Facebook at LeeCaraher1.

www.LeeCaraher.com

@LeeCaraher

LeeCaraher1